THE
RED ARROWS

Trailing white smoke, the team passes over the top of a loop and heads down towards the Mediterranean. This view is from Red 2, immediately to the right of the leader.

THE
RED ARROWS

Chris Bennett

SUTTON PUBLISHING

First published in 2003 by
Sutton Publishing Limited · Phoenix Mill
Thrupp · Stroud · Gloucestershire · GL5 2BU

British Library Cataloguing in Publication Data
A catalogue record for this book is available from the British Library.

ISBN 0-7509-3096-9

Title page photograph: The Diamond Nine, the Red Arrows' elegant 'trademark' formation.

Dedication

To my beautiful little daughter Georgina Joan

Typeset in 10/14pt Sabon.
Typesetting and origination by
Sutton Publishing Limited.
Printed and bound in England by
J.H. Haynes & Co. Ltd, Sparkford.

Contents

The Red Arrows' display lasts twenty-two minutes. For the first half of it all nine aircraft fly together to demonstrate the various formation shapes in a series of bends, turns and loops. For the second half of the display the team splits into two packages, the front five, 'Enid', behind the team leader, and the rear four, 'Gypo', which includes the dynamic Synchro Pair. To achieve the break during poor weather with a low cloud base, the team uses the 5/4 cross as seen here.

Introduction

This book is the culmination of several years' work with the Red Arrows. It was made possible because of the incredible degree of access the team allowed me to their activities, both on the ground and in the air. The book is also the culmination of a dream. I first worked with the Red Arrows in 1997, after three years of knocking at their door. Having flown in many military fast jets without mishap, I felt I had served my apprenticeship in aerial photography. For me, an opportunity to work with the finest, the best of the best, was an ambition I needed to fulfil.

Finally, I did get to fly with the team. From tentative, nervous beginnings, I have now logged over 100 flights with them. It is an honour to fly with the Red Arrows, for few outsiders are permitted to do so. It is an even greater honour to be accepted by the team and to gain their trust. Over the years I have come to know many members of the team personally. Moreover, the more I understand about how the Red Arrows do what they do, the more I admire them. They are truly among the finest aviators in the world.

As well as describing the Royal Air Force Aerobatic Team and how it operates, in this book I try to explain how they perform their formation aerobatics. If I have done my job well, this should enhance the reader's enjoyment of the team's display and will increase the understanding of what it is like up there, twisting, turning, looping and rolling. As I look at some of my images, they now seem so sedate and 'flat' on paper. Then I remember what it was like to take them – and it was not sedate, take my word for it!

The majority of the imagery in this book is taken from the air. However, there are also several shots taken on the ground, which I hope put a human face on the Red Arrows' team members. The pictures range in date from those taken during my first experience with the Reds in 1997 to several taken during the 2002 season.

For those interested, all the imagery was produced using Nikon cameras and lenses: a lightweight F90 for air-to-air use and a brace of F5 cameras for use on the ground. The rear-facing pictures, looking backwards at the team leader (with me in the rear cockpit), were produced using a remote-mounted 16mm lens fitted to an old Nikon F801 camera. For most of the air-to-air images I used a 35–70mm zoom lens, as well as an 80–200mm zoom, a 20mm and a 16mm lens. Most ground pictures were taken using a 20mm or an 80–200mm lens, plus others with a 16mm, a 35–70mm zoom or a 300mm lens. Film stock was always 35mm transparency, principally Kodak Elitechrome Extra Colour and Fuji Velvia or Provia. Ceta of Poland Street, London, processed the films.

Red 3, to the left of the leader, in his element – the vertical!

CHAPTER 1
Predecessors

The art of formation flying is almost as old as aviation itself, and the ability to fly in close proximity to other planes has been taught to military pilots from the First World War to the present day. Why? Well apart from the pure flying skill, formation flying is the only way for multiples of aircraft to take off and land quickly, and for sections of aircraft to penetrate cloud. The ability to fly aerobatics is also a fundamental flying skill. In addition to the direct relevance to aerial combat, the ability to fly accurate aerobatics confers on pilots the confidence to fly their aircraft to the limits of its performance envelope.

Given the importance of formation flying and aerobatics in the training of military pilots, it could not be long before these elements were combined to provide a spectacular display at air shows. There was hard-nosed reasoning behind this seeming frivolity. During the 1920s and the early 1930s the Royal Air Force had to fight hard to preserve its independence. Part of that fight centred on a sustained campaign to instil air-mindedness in the British public. This was achieved by a series of publicity stunts such as record-breaking flights to distant points on the globe, and the setting of new speed and altitude records.

Another important aspect of that publicity effort was the Royal Air Force Tournament and its successors, the Royal Air Force Pageant and the Royal Air Force Display, held at RAF Hendon on the northern outskirts of London. The first of them was staged in 1920 and the last in 1937. In the following year the Munich Crisis, rearmament and the gathering war clouds brought an end to the annual event.

Feats of aerial skill and daring-do were an integral part of the Hendon displays. During the 1920 display five Sopwith Snipe fighters from the Central Flying School looped and rolled in formation and flew inverted. In 1926 nine Siskin fighters from 41 Squadron performed aerobatics and formation changes to music. Such formation displays became common, though their range of manoeuvres fell far short of those which modern aircraft can undertake. During the 1936 display three Gloster Gauntlet biplane fighters of 19 Squadron performed close-formation aerobatics with their wings tied together using breakable cord.

The Hendon air displays during the interwar years were a huge success on three levels. First, by keeping the RAF in the public eye, they helped ensure that the service enjoyed a powerful and supportive air lobby both in the country and in Parliament. Secondly, they helped generate a pool of air enthusiasts keen to volunteer for the service. That huge fund of goodwill created for the service between the wars would greatly assist its expansion when war became inevitable. And thirdly, the air displays raised morale in the service and heightened its image of itself and its abilities.

After 1945 the RAF resumed its programme of air displays. These took place at airfields throughout the country each September, to commemorate the Battle of Britain. In the years that followed almost every self-respecting RAF fighter squadron possessed its own formation air display team. With the introduction of the fast and manoeuvrable Canberra, some jet bomber units also joined in.

In the late 1950s the practice of letting front-line squadrons form their own formation aerobatic teams gave way to the selection of a single fighter squadron to perform at the most prestigious venues. In 1957 that honour went to 111 Squadron, which put on an exciting show at the Farnborough Air Display using nine Hawker Hunter fighters. Ever larger display teams were now the order of the day – a process that reached its climax at the same venue in the following year when 111 Squadron's team, the Black Arrows, employed sixteen black-painted Hunters for the main part of its performance. Then, in an unforgettable finale, they were joined by six Hunters of 56 Squadron for the audacious feat of looping twenty-two Hunters in tight formation.

During the early 1960s the Hunter was replaced by the supersonic Lightning in the RAF's home defence fighter squadrons. In the 1962 Farnborough Air Show 74 Squadron's aerobatic team, The Tigers, gave an impressively noisy display using nine Lightnings. It was magnificent, but it was too good to last. The Lightning was much more complex and expensive than its predecessors, and it was also much more demanding to fly. The diversion of a front-line fighter squadron away from its normal combat flying training tasks, in order to work up a team to display standard, was a burden that became increasingly difficult to justify.

Accordingly, in 1964 the Air Council ruled that front-line fighter units were no longer to undertake that task. In future only training units would be permitted to create formation aerobatic teams, using instructor pilots. In that year the Red Pelicans, with five Jet Provost basic training aircraft based at RAF Hullavington, became an official aerobatic team, and the Yellowjacks, flying five yellow-painted Folland Gnat advanced jet-trainers, formed at RAF Valley. The small, fast and manoeuvrable Gnat proved a far superior display vehicle than the Jet Provost, and in 1965 a new aerobatic team was formed: The Red Arrows.

CHAPTER 2

Making it Happen

RED ARROWS PAST AND PRESENT

In May 1965, with Flight Lieutenant Lee Jones as team leader and operating seven Gnat advanced training aircraft, the Red Arrows gave their first public display at the Biggin Hill International Fair. It was a resounding success. Increasing their popularity by the year, from mid-1966 the Red Arrows flew as a nine-plane team and they have retained that number ever since.

The Red Arrows operated Gnats until 1979, and during their fourteen years with this aircraft they flew 1,292 public displays. By then, however, the Gnat was passing out of RAF service. So for the 1980 season the Red Arrows re-equipped with the RAF's latest advanced jet-trainer, the British Aerospace Hawk. Powered by a single Rolls-Royce Adour turbofan developing 5,200lb-thrust, the two-seat Hawk is a highly manoeuvrable aircraft that has proved ideal for low-level formation aerobatics. The aircraft has served the team well for more than a couple of decades, and has plenty of life left in it yet.

Currently the Red Arrows' home base is at RAF Scampton in Lincolnshire, the airfield from which the Avro Lancaster bombers of 617 Squadron took off to deliver their epic attack on the Ruhr dams in May 1943. For anyone visiting Scampton and interested in the airfield's history, lunch at the Dambusters Arms public house in

A glance inside the front office of a Red Arrows Hawk reveals that by modern standards the cockpit is relatively old and basic. In front of the pilot is his pitch map with the datum marked upon it, bracketed by the angled lines the team will use during the display. That makes it easier to pick out the landmarks on the ground. To the right, tucked into the cockpit coaming, is a set of maps ready for the transit flight to the next display site.

The twin cockpit layout of the Hawk. In the rear seat the man in the standard green helmet is a short-listed prospective pilot hoping to join the team. Each year only three new pilots are chosen, or two during a year when the leader changes.

Scampton village is highly recommended. One wall of the lounge is covered with a fascinating collection of memorabilia depicting aspects of the airfield's past. And the food is good, too!

In 1995, reluctantly and as an economy measure, the RAF planned to close the airfield at Scampton. As a prelude to that closure, for the 1996 display season the Red Arrows moved to RAF Cranwell some 20 miles to the south. The relocation proved difficult, however, owing to the team's unique requirements.

Cranwell is an extremely busy flying training airfield in its own right, and there are other training and operational bases in its immediate area. While the team continued to use the reserved airspace above Scampton for the majority of its training, six times a day the formations had to take off from and land at Cranwell, requiring other movements to cease during that period. In addition a number of training slots were actually flown at Cranwell, with a paralysing effect on the station's normal flying training activities.

Squadron Leader Spike Jepson boards his
Hawk as he prepares for another sortie.
Although the Hawk is not a high-
performance jet, its single Rolls-Royce
Adour turbofan gives it a sprightly edge.

A Hawk is towed from its hangar at RAF
Cranwell for the first sortie of the day.

Although Scampton was theoretically closed, during each practice display the air traffic control tower needed to be manned. The emergency fire and rescue services also had to be in place in case of a mishap. Furthermore, the runway and taxiways at Scampton needed to be maintained in a serviceable condition, in case an aircraft needed to put down there. In the end it was decided to reopen Scampton and base the Red Arrows there permanently. With most of its facilities closed, the airfield resembles a ghost town. But that solitude is ideal for the Red Arrows, who can carry out their programme of flying training without suffering interference – or causing it to anyone else.

PILOT SELECTION AND TRAINING

The Red Arrows formation team consists of nine pilots, known by their radio callsigns as Reds 1 to 9. The tenth pilot, Red 10, acts as the team's road manager, display commentator and flight safety officer. Most pilots selected for the Red Arrows serve with the team for three years. The major exception is the team leader, Red 1. After flying with the team for a three-year stint as a wingman, an experienced pilot is selected and invited to lead the team for the next three years.

At the end of each year's display season, the three pilots who have completed their third year leave to resume their RAF careers. In their place will come three new pilots for the next display season. Thus in each year at least six of the team's members will be old hands, providing a valuable core of experience.

The selection and recruitment of new pilots for the Red Arrows is a serious business. Typically, a volunteer will be in his late twenties or early thirties, and nearing the end of his second operational flying tour. He will have at least 1,500 flying hours under his belt, and will

Squadron Leader Andy Cubin climbs aboard his Hawk at Cranwell.

Squadron Leader (now Wing Commander) Andy Offer dons his helmet. He led the team during the 2000 and 2001 display seasons. Usually team leaders remain in post for three years, but Andy's tenure was cut short owing to promotion.

Fired up and ready to go. Beneath Andy Offer's name on the cockpit side is that of Flight Lieutenant Tim Beagle, the team's Junior Engineering Officer. During the display season the latter flies in the leader's rear seat to the various forward operating locations.

have about five years' service with front-line units operating Jaguars, Tornados or Harriers.

Each year the team usually receives more than thirty applications from pilots wanting to join. Of those, nine are short-listed. The short-listing process starts with an examination of each pilot's confidential record of his service flying. This frank-speaking document lists the flying abilities and, where applicable, the failings of each pilot. The team leader looks for pilots rated as 'above average', who have shown a consistent trend of improvement. Other requirements are the ability to learn quickly, to work well as part of a team, to get on well with others socially and to show enthusiasm for the job. Despite the high standard of the applicants, not everybody will possess the maturity, coolness under pressure and self-discipline that are essential in this job.

During the selection process the views of the current team members play an important part.

While a member of the groundcrew secures the wheel chocks, Flight Lieutenant Justin Hughes, the 2002 Team Executive Officer, dismounts. In his third and last year with the team, Justin flies Red 9, one of the most dynamic slots. In many ways the third year with the team is the best, because by then a pilot is familiar with the flying and can, to some extent, sit back and enjoy it.

The RAF's Jaguar, Tornado and Harrier forces are small, close-knit communities, so at least one team member will have personal knowledge of any pilot who applies to join the Red Arrows. A personal recommendation for an applicant from an existing member of the team is taken seriously, as is a reasoned rejection. From the thirty or so applications submitted, the team select the nine they think will be best suited for the job.

Each year, during April and the early part of May, the Red Arrows move to RAF Akrotiri in Cyprus for their annual period of four weeks' intensive flying training. At that time of the year the weather at Akrotiri is ideal, with clear blue skies allowing the Reds to practise the new display routine again and again until it becomes second nature. The nine short-listed pilots go to Akrotiri

The Red Arrows generally spend the bulk of April at RAF Akrotiri in Cyprus, taking advantage of the consistently good weather there to put the final polish on their display. Each day they fly three practice displays. After the last practice of the day the hard-working technicians carry out their maintenance tasks, in this case the replacement of a main wheel tyre.

Opposite: The Red Arrows' distinctive scarlet Hawk jets look resplendent as they sit in line on the sun-bleached pan at Akrotiri. Between practice display sorties the jets are refuelled. To keep down their weight and so reduce airframe fatigue, the jets take off with partially filled tanks. For a display over the base airfield, each Hawk is loaded with 950lb of fuel.

Before each display there is a thorough briefing. As the jets sitting on the line await their pilots, the latter discuss in detail the objectives of their next flight. As well as looking at ways to perfect the display, the leader points out the specifics of this particular display datum.

with the team, and during rehearsals they fly in the rear seats of the Hawks to see what is involved.

There are three elements to the short-list week: an interview, a flying test and social time. The interview is to some extent a test of maturity, to check that the new pilot will cope with the media and PR aspects of the job. The flying test is a check of the individual's ability in pure formation flying. And as long as the other two elements have gone well, probably the most important

facet is the social time. There is no magic formula to 'fitting in'; the team includes a cross-section of personalities. However, it is important that new members will adapt to and cope with the Red Arrows' environment.

Although it is just one part of the selection process, the flying test tends to figure prominently in the candidates' minds. The test is flown with the team's executive officer in the front seat of the Hawk and the prospective pilot flying from the

12

Still in Cyprus but sporting a different pair of shades, Squadron Leader Spike Jepson, the 'Boss', in full cry during a Cyprus-based pre-practice briefing.

Synchro Lead Jas Hawker (right) and Synchro Two Myles Garland study an aerial photograph of the next display datum, one of several in use around Akrotiri.

Squadron Leader Andy Offer boards his Hawk for yet another practice display. During their pre-season training the Red Arrows' pilots wear standard green flight suits. They get their distinctive scarlet suits when the team receives its annual licence to display in public.

Everything to do with the Red Arrows is precise, and that includes parking the aircraft. When the Hawks return from their sortie they are lined up, inch perfect. At Akrotiri there are few watching the performance, but during the display season the team operates under close public scrutiny and so they need to train as they intend to perform.

15

Main picture: For a photographer privileged to fly with the Red Arrows, the annual detachment to Cyprus is the ideal chance to take air-to-air pictures of the team in action. For me, some of the most stunning shots are those showing the pristine red-and-white jets against the deep blue of the Mediterranean.

Above: This is a similar view taken from within the formation, from Red 4, while flying in Big Vixen. The wing-tips of the jets are just a few feet apart.

rear seat. He has to maintain close formation on the team leader as he performs four loops then four barrel rolls in succession. Those two manoeuvres form the basis of most of the team's aerobatics. As well as observing the pilot's ability to hold formation accurately and smoothly, the team leader looks for signs that the pilot can learn quickly from any errors and can improve his performance from one manoeuvre to the next.

Following the Akrotiri detachment, the prospective pilots return to their units. Meanwhile the team leader and members discuss each man's abilities, and his suitability for the unit. The three best applicants are then chosen, and

The nine-ship Red Arrows formation pulls up into the vertical during a loop. This manoeuvre eats up about 6,000ft of airspace. In the background is the resort town of Limassol, popular with British tourists.

18

informed of their selection. In August each new pilot leaves his current unit and goes on a refresher flying course on the Hawk at RAF Valley. The new pilots are then posted to the Red Arrows, and accompany the team during the final weeks of the display season. This gives them a clear idea of the day-to-day running of the team, before they join it as full members for the next year.

Once the display season finishes at the end of September, most of the team depart for three weeks of well-earned leave – there is no time for leave during the season itself. This slack period gives the team leader time to start training his new pilots, each of whom will already have been assigned a position in the formation.

Unless a new pilot has performed display aerobatics previously, it is unlikely he will have performed loops or rolls that take him below the RAF's regulation minimum height of 5,000ft above ground level. During the next few weeks

Much of the land bordering Akrotiri is barren and brown, a world away from the lush green of the Red Arrows' home base at RAF Scampton.

19

the team leader flies with the new pilots two or three times a day, to build up their close-formation flying skills. He also makes a step-by-step reduction in the display height until the newcomers can confidently perform manoeuvres within 300ft of the ground. By the time the rest of the team return from leave, the new members will be ready to take their places in the formation and can perform reasonably well, though their flying will lack polish.

During the winter the team works up three types of display, full, flat and rolling, although any individual show may be a combination of manoeuvres from all three routines, as conditions vary on the day. Full manoeuvres are flown when cloud conditions allow loops up to around 6,000ft above the ground; rolling manoeuvres require a cloud base above approximately 2,500ft; and flat manoeuvres are flown when low cloud prevents manoeuvres with any vertical extent. The work-up phase of the training culminates in the detachment to Akrotiri already described. By now the team is flying its full nine-ship display, with regular practices to give it that final polish.

The profile for every sortie throughout the training period follows a similar pattern. Every RAF sortie begins with a thorough pre-flight briefing. The Red Arrows' pre-season briefings cover a large amount of training information as well as stressing safety points. The in-season briefings concentrate more on navigational points and items of flight safety information relevant to the particular venue, although points from the last display are always reviewed. The datum point for the display – that point on which the display will be centred – is marked on maps and photographs of the display venue.

Every sortie performed by the Red Arrows, whether for practice or before the public, is video-recorded for subsequent analysis. This is particularly valuable during the early stages of

The shadows on the ground show that Enid section is flying at low altitude. Before they join the team most Red Arrows' pilots will have had some experience of low flying, though not of flying aerobatic manoeuvres in tight formation. Normally RAF pilots are not permitted to perform aerobatic manoeuvres that take them below 5,000ft. New pilots joining the team first need to get used to manoeuvring at progressively lower altitudes, until they can do so confidently at a minimum of 300ft above the ground.

Flight Lieutenant Jason 'Jas' Hawker, Red 6, tucks his Hawk in close during the first half of the display. In the rear seat is one of the nine short-listed pilots, from whom the team's three new pilots for the 2003 display season were selected. This will be Jas's last year with the team, before he returns to a front-line Tornado squadron.

The Red Arrows taxi out for a pre-season practice display. The tenth jet is a borrowed aircraft, to make up the numbers while some of the team's complement of twelve Hawks are undergoing inspection.

training, but it continues to be useful throughout the season in the team's quest for perfection. The filming is done by a member of the Red Arrows' groundcrew, who is located at the display's datum point. As soon as possible after each display, while the details are still fresh in the pilots' minds, the video is shown during the post-flight debriefing.

Like the pre-flight briefing, the post-flight de-briefing is standard RAF practice. These are always directed at finding answers for the same three questions: 'What, if anything, went wrong?'; 'How can we prevent that happening again?'; and 'How can we fly the mission better next time?' Even when a display looked superb to spectators, in the ultra-critical eyes of the leader and the team members it is unlikely to have been 'perfect' in every respect. There are always lessons to learn. The Red Arrows aim for perfec-

Flight Lieutenant John Green, complete with *de rigueur* shades (if there is the merest possibility of sunshine you will not see a Red Arrows' team member without them!), concentrates on the pre-display briefing. John joined the RAF in 1987 and spent three tours flying Jaguar fighters with 54 Squadron at Coltishall in Norfolk. He was selected for the Red Arrows in 2002 and will fly as Red 5 during the 2003 season.

There's nothing like a good yawn to blow away the pre-briefing cobwebs – is there, DT? Dave Thomas will take over the coveted Red 7 slot from Myles Garland for the 2003 season, while Myles moves to Red 6, Synchro Lead.

The great thing about Cyprus is that it offers an extensive range of backgrounds for pictures. Some, like this one, resemble a lunar landscape.

Squadron Leader Spike Jepson, Red 1, leads the team as it banks over Akrotiri. To Spike's left (to the right in the picture) are Reds 3 and 5 and to his right Reds 2 and 4. The even numbers are always on the right of the formation and the odd numbers on the left. Reds 6 and 7 trail the leader in the centreline 'stem'.

tion. Of course, absolute perfection throughout every moment of every display is impossible to achieve – but, through progressive, unrelenting practice and continual analysis and attention to detail, the display will appear perfect to the observer on the ground.

Having completed the training, there remains one last but very important hurdle for the team to jump. It must gain its Public Display Authority, the annually renewable licence without which the team cannot display before the public. The examination takes place towards the end of the detachment at Akrotiri when the team performs its display before the Commander-in-Chief of RAF Personnel and Training Command. His job is to check that the display is of the expected standard, and that it contains no element that could put either pilots or spectators at risk. If he

is unhappy with anything, the officer has the power to refuse authority for the team to perform. Thankfully, nobody has yet felt it necessary to invoke that power.

Once the team has gained its Public Display Authority, each pilot receives his tailored, bright red flight suit for the coming season. That indicates he has met all the exacting membership requirements for the world's most exclusive flying club, the Red Arrows.

THE SUPPORT TEAM

The nine display pilots with the road manager are the stars of the show, but one must never forget that for each of them there are eight men or women working in support. In the headquarters are the team manager, public relations officer and adjutant. Furthermore, in addition to its complement of sixty-five technicians to keep the aircraft serviceable, the team has two flight-planning clerks, an admin support team, safety equipment specialists and drivers. Collectively they are known as the 'Blues', because of the tailored blue overalls they wear during the display season.

Commanding the Blues are two engineering officers, the Senior Engineering Officer with the rank of squadron leader, and the Junior Engineering Officer with the rank of flight lieutenant. In recognition of their status, both engineering officers and the team manager are eligible to wear the same coveted red flight suits as the pilots.

During the display season the Red Arrows' groundcrews are worked hard, but none more so than members of the 'Circus', the ten individuals who fly to the forward operating bases in the rear seats of the Hawks. The Circus members are chosen in such a way as to provide a cross-section of the trade skills needed to remedy those technical snags likely to arise when away from base. Despite the hard work involved, there is never any shortage of volunteers for positions in the Circus. As well as flying regularly, these technicians have a well-deserved share in the Red Arrows' celebrity status at many of the air shows.

During the display season the Red Arrows often operate away from Scampton. When more than one display is required away from base, a

With the Red Arrows' distinctive red flight suits comes instant celebrity status. Wherever the pilots go, when attired in the easily recognisable suits they are mobbed by autograph hunters of all ages. Do not be misled by Gleavie Gleave's cool demeanour – he loves the limelight!

25-strong ground support party goes to the forward operating base. In the United Kingdom the support party usually travels by road but for deployments overseas the support party and its equipment are carried by Hercules transport plane.

The Red Arrows' year is divided into two quite separate parts, and the division is significant in terms of the engineering commitment. There is the summer and autumn air show period, throughout which the pilots and aircraft need to be tuned for top performance. Then there is the winter and spring period, when the aircraft undergo their planned inspections and overhauls, and the support staff can take leave due to them. During this time at least four aircraft are always kept serviceable, to allow pilot training to continue. The aim is to have nine or ten Hawks serviceable at the end of February, before the first nine-ship formation of the year, and to have all twelve aircraft ready at the end of March for the Cyprus detachment.

During the display season the team usually launches from Scampton with ten Hawks, the nine display participants plus a spare flown by Red 10, the road manager. To be certain of achieving that number, the team needs to have eleven or preferably all twelve of its aircraft serviceable.

Another problem that needs to be taken into account by the engineers is the cumulative fatigue to the airframe caused by pulling large amounts of g during manoeuvres. Each RAF aircraft carries a fatigue meter, which registers the amount of the aircraft's life which is used up each time it flies. In the Red Arrows nos 6, 7, 8 and 9 generate significantly greater fatigue levels than Nos 1 to 5, owing to the dynamic nature of their manoeuvres during the show. The aircraft are therefore allocated to display positions which ensure that over a couple of display seasons the amount of airframe fatigue is evenly spread across the fleet.

For each display season each Hawk is assigned to a particular pilot whose name is painted on the port side below the cockpit. Apart from adding a personal touch, this arrangement allows each pilot to become accustomed to the foibles of his particular aircraft. Seemingly trivial variations between aircraft can introduce unique handling qualities.

Apart from the distinctive colour scheme, the main external difference between the standard Hawk and the Red Arrows' machines is the smoke pod mounted under the fuselage. This streamlined unit houses three separate tanks. One contains 50 gallons of neat diesel oil, which is injected into the hot engine efflux to produce a white smoke trail. The other two tanks each hold 10 gallons of a mixture of diesel oil and red or blue industrial dye, to produce trails in those colours.

The 50 gallons of neat diesel oil provide five minutes of white smoke, while the red and blue tanks provide sufficient for only one minute's running for each of these colours. Those limitations have to be considered when designing the display, since the highly visual ribbons of smoke are an essential element of it.

Having looked at some of the organisation that supports the flying, let us now look at the flying itself.

CHAPTER 3

Close-Formation Aerobatics

WHAT'S IT ALL ABOUT?

Formation flying has been around almost as long as flying itself; well, at least since the development of the second flying machine. As a pure flying skill, it is both challenging and fun; it also has many operational uses though: take-off and landing for large formations, cloud penetration, mutual support and so on. However, modern aircraft capabilities and tactics mean that there is no longer any tactical requirement for close-formation flying; it is just one of the tools in a pilot's bag of tricks to be taken out on an occasional basis when required. So even for an experienced fighter pilot, formation aerobatics is a new skill to learn.

No matter what their previous experience or apparent disdain for those guys 'posing in red suits', most fighter pilots' first impression of sitting in the back seat during a Red Arrows' sortie is that the experience is somewhere between awesome, crazy and very impressive. It's not until you're pulling out of a loop vertically nose down at 4000ft with eight other aircraft bobbing around you that you really start to appreciate what's involved. So how does it work?

Well, the concept of formation flying is fairly simple. It's just a case of drawing out two imaginary lines from an aircraft and trying to stay in the position where the lines meet. On the diagram below, there's one line extended out along the front edge of the wing and one coming out along the front edge of the tailplane. Where they meet defines a specific point and the skill is just to stay at that point. In reality, you would

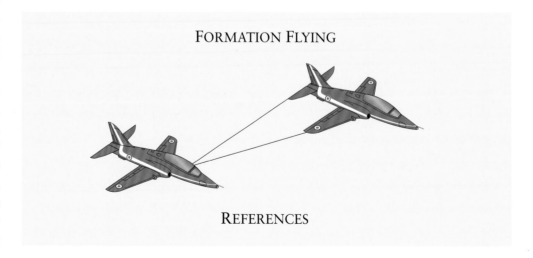

FORMATION FLYING

REFERENCES

The Mediterranean again serves as a backdrop for one of my all-time favourite shots of the Red Arrows. The formation is Leader's Benefit, during which Reds 2, 3, 4 and 5 are in line abreast, with Red 1 slightly in front. I particularly like the rim light catching the top of the canopies, separating them from the dark sea. This is not one of the most dramatic pictures of the team, but the mixture of colours is outstanding.

A formation take-off, seen from Red 9. The aircraft nearest the camera is Red 8, formating on Red 6.

The Red Arrows lift off from Scampton's runway using their standard display take-off. The team leader heads Reds 2 and 3 in 'vic', with Reds 4 and 5 some 750ft behind, and Reds 6, 7, 8 and 9 a further 750ft behind them.

The team trains regularly during the pre-season build-up. If a pilot falls ill and cannot fly, the rest of the team continue to practise without him. During work-up for the 1997 season Dave Stobie, Red 7, hurt his neck and was grounded for a spell. Fortunately, the absence of his aircraft from the rear of the formation could be worked around. The resultant eight-ship Diamond formation looked quite good, too!

The 1998 team heads 'for the weeds' during a practice display over Scampton. Close-formation flying is achieved by lining up reference points on the jet on which one is formating. This picture was taken from Red 4, one of whose references is to align Red 2's head – in the nearest jet – with that of the team leader in the furthest jet. I was flying in Red 4's rear seat. Note that the passengers' heads in Red 1 and Red 2 are virtually in line. In fact, we were slightly high when the picture was taken, because we should not be able to see quite so much of the leader's canopy.

The view from the rear seat as we looped behind the leader and Synchro Lead. To avoid the jet efflux we were stepped down below, as well as behind, Red 6. He in turn was below and behind Red 1.

also have some sort of depth reference to confirm that you are at the right level vertically. And that's all there is to it!

There are four basic formation positions used in the display: arrow, diamond, line abreast and line astern. Arrow and diamond are traditional formation positions as in the diagram on the right, differentiated only by the closeness between the aircraft. Line abreast is when the aircraft are side by side and is the most difficult position to fly because it is very difficult to assess changes in the distance between the aircraft. Line astern is, as you would imagine, when the aircraft are one behind the other, each a little lower than the one in front to remain clear of the jetwash.

The Red Arrows use a variety of formation references to define all the different positions which make up the formation shapes. Although the team do use a line along the wing, they also

The Red Arrows roll in Flanker formation, one of those used during the 1997 season in tribute to the Russian Su-27 fighter. Each year it is the team leader's prerogative to modify the display to keep it fresh and different. Usually there is something new in it to thrill the crowds.

The team loops in Flanker in typical British weather. While a dull cloudy day might allow enough room for the full display, it is certainly not ideal for photography. The pictures are simply not as good as those taken when the sun is out. Dull weather regularly parks itself over Scampton during practice displays; frustratingly, it almost always clears away within an hour of landing!

use the gap above the teddy bear's ear (an air vent on the top of the aircraft), the extent to which various nuts and bolts are obscured, and the paintwork on the aircraft (including one bit of paintwork added for just this purpose). Other variations are also used, including positions where references are taken off two different

aircraft. However, the concept never changes. In every case the principle is the same: to hold the aircraft at the intersection of two lines in the horizontal plane, at the same time as staying at the correct height.

This description outlines the situation for Reds 2 and 3, who fly next to the leader, and for Red 6 who flies mainly in line astern. The situation is a little more complicated for Reds 4, 5, 7, 8 and 9, who each have other aircraft between them and Red 1. In this case, the same principle applies but in a slightly different way. They take one reference from the aircraft closest to them and draw another line (or reference) by lining up the leader's head with the head of the pilot in the aircraft next to them.

The formation positions in Diamond are shown on p. 39. The logic of the numbering is the same for all the formations, with even numbers on the right, odd numbers on the left. The lower numbers (less experienced in the team) are towards the front. The Synchro Pair (Reds 6 and 7) generally fly behind Red 1.

THE LEADER'S ROLE

So once you know where you're supposed to be, the clever bit is to stay there. The first thing to think about is the role of the leader. Red 1's job is multi-faceted but one of his most important tasks is to provide a stable reference for everybody else to formate on. To that end, he will attempt to be completely predictable, using exactly the same inputs to roll and pitch the aircraft every time. Over time, the wingmen (everybody else) get so used to Red 1's actions that they instinctively put in the correct inputs to maintain their own position during a manoeuvre. Also, all of the leader's inputs are called on the radio. For instance, at the start of a loop, the leader calls

All eyes are on us as Red 3 formates off the leader while Red 5, outboard of Red 3, does the same. The triangle made by Reds 1, 2 and 3 forms the foundation of the Red Arrows' multi-jet formations. It is imperative that Red 2 and Red 3 keep station on the leader accurately and consistently, because the other jets formate on them.

Well, there's a contented-looking Red Arrow.
The trouble is, I'm not really sure *which* Red
Arrow lies beneath all that hardware!
Answers on a postcard please . . .

Red 10 – spot the give-away '10' reflected off his helmet in the canopy – follows the other nine Red Arrows out for an aerial photography chase sortie.

As the team bends to the left in Diamond Nine, Red 10 tries hard to catch up. That's easier said than done, as the aircraft in front are probably going flat out, leaving us little in reserve to overtake them. All those air-to-air pictures showing the nine-jet formations are taken from Red 10's aircraft. His job is demanding. Not only must he get me, the photographer, to the right place at the right time to capture the image, but he also needs to be mindful of what the team is doing to avoid compromising safety.

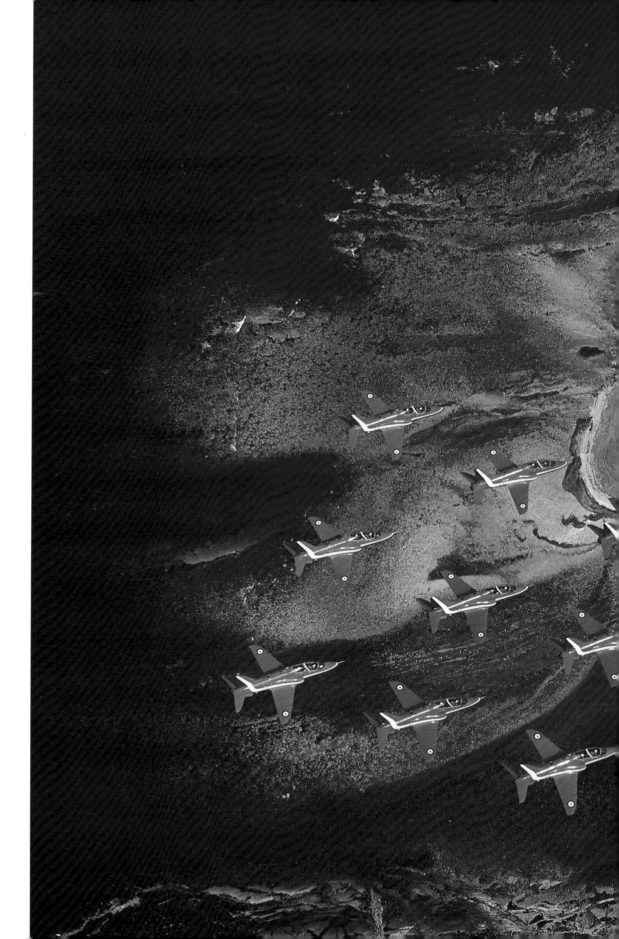

En route to Scampton from RAF Kinloss, the team forms up in Diamond Nine for some set-up pictures off the coast, courtesy of Red 10.

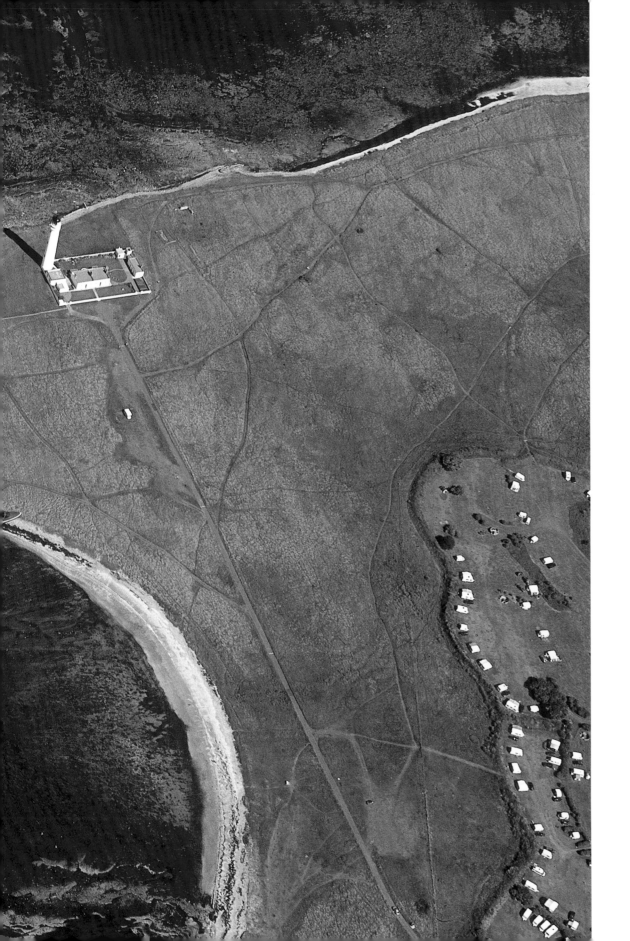

'Pulling <u>Up</u>' with the emphasis on the 'U' of 'Up'. Exactly on that syllable, he pulls the control column back to start the loop. His aim is to allow everybody to commence the pull-up at exactly the same time, rather than for them to react to his movement. The principle is particularly important for the outside positions, who may have only a very limited view of the leader. However, they will still take all their cues from Red 1 and from his radio calls.

Red 1 will literally call every movement of the control column or throttle that he makes, in order to allow everybody else to adjust simultaneously. However, no system is perfect and you can imagine the chaos during a training sortie when the leader called 'coming left now' and proceeded to bank to the right. The most amusing aspect was that he accidentally kept the radio transmit button selected during the stream of expletives which immediately followed as he realised his mistake!

TECHNIQUES

So the aim is to stay in the same position relative to the leader. The basic technique to achieve this is to get in the correct position on one reference, i.e. to be on one of those lines, and then move up or down that line until you can see the second reference. Of course, in practice an experienced pilot will correct to both references simultaneously. Power (via the throttle) is used to move forwards and back with the airbrake being used occasionally during position changes. The control column is used in the same sense as for 'normal' flying to move the aircraft up, down, left and right. And all these things happen at once. So you can see there's a lot to think about in just maintaining position before you start doing aerobatics. When you start manoeuvring it all gets a bit more complicated.

The aircraft will tend to bounce around a bit and the trick is to ignore everyone else's movements apart from Red 1. This can be difficult, especially on a windy day. Probably the best example of this is in Apollo formation. Apollo is the closest formation which the team flies, with the jets approximately 10ft from one another, wingtip to wingtip. Reds 8 and 9 fly this formation immediately behind but around 10ft lower than Reds 2 and 3. However, their references are solely from Red 1. The pilots do not even look at the jets right in front of and next to them! It takes a lot of practice and trust to ignore the movement of the other jets, but that's the only way to avoid huge ripples through the formation.

The other skill in manoeuvring is anticipation. Some manoeuvres require big inputs of power or movement and if you wait until you can

Off the Cyprus coast the team rolls in Concorde formation as Red 10, Steve Underwood, puts me in the right place at the right time. Getting a good picture requires teamwork. Although I hold the camera, compose the picture and press the shutter, the image I get depends entirely on where Steve puts me.

47

With streamers spiralling from their wing-tips, the Hawks pull out of a loop. The streamers are generated when the aircraft manoeuvre in air with a high moisture content.

Heading for the weeds!

see that you need the input, then it is almost certainly too late. The best example of this is in the rolls. When we talk about a roll in formation aerobatics, we actually mean a barrel roll, as if rolling the formation around the outside of a barrel. With nine aircraft in the formation, the inputs required to hold position for the outside jets (normally Reds 8 and 9 for the rolls) are huge. At the start of a roll to the left, Red 9 has to push hard down, roll and reduce power at the same time. However, halfway around the roll, more power is required and it is necessary to slam the throttle to full power long before the requirement

is obvious, owing to the wind-up time of a jet engine. Red 8 has the opposite sequence of events: pull up, roll and increase power at the start, with power reducing during the roll. The difficulty in flying rolls for both the leader and the wingmen means that these manoeuvres are only ever flown in one direction (currently to the left).

FLYING THE SHOW – THE FIRST HALF

The display is essentially in two halves. During the first half all nine jets remain together and perform a sequence of manoeuvres in different formation shapes. In the second half the formation splits into three sections for a coordinated sequence of more dynamic manoeuvres.

While the formation skills previously discussed are common to all the team's flying, there are some techniques which are peculiar to each half of the show. During the first half it is solely Red 1's responsibility to position the formation in front of the crowd and to control all the formation changes. Everybody else simply flies their formation references the whole time, although the Synchro Pair will probably try to sneak a quick look at the features of the display site in preparation for the second half.

In any formation shape the pilots are using exactly the formation skills described previously.

The moves between the different formations are all called by Red 1 and acknowledged by the pilots of those aircraft who move the furthest or whose move affects another aircraft. These moves are sometimes complex with a second radio call halfway through to initiate a second move. An example from the 2002 show was the move between Big Vixen and Short Diamond. The radio sequence was:

Red 1:	'Short Diamond Go'
Response:	'6, 7, Go, 8, 9'
Red 9:	'Smoke off Go'

In this move, on the leader's 'Go', 8 and 9 turn their smoke on. Reds 6 and 7 acknowledge the

The dark Mediterranean provides a splendidly contrasting backdrop for the Red Arrows as they roll in Wineglass formation. From this angle it is not easy to see which formation they are in. Although it might not appear so, the five rear aircraft are in 'vic' and the front three are in line abreast, the two elements being linked by Red 6.

Going down!

The Red Arrows pull down, entering the last quarter of a loop during an in-season practice from Scampton. If the team has not flown its display for more than five days, prior to performing in public it needs a practice display to bring its performance up to scratch.

The daring passes by the Synchro Pair are one of the trademarks of the Red Arrows. Although in reality the two jets have about 100ft between them when they pass, at their combined closing speed of more than 800 miles per hour that is quite dramatic enough!

The Synchro Pair go head-to-head on a cloudy day at Nancy in France. This job is the most coveted within the Red Arrows, since the flying is the most dramatic. One bonus of having served in the Synchro Pair is that it marks out a pilot as a potential team leader. Nearly all the Red Arrows' leaders have served at one time in the Synchro Pair.

call and move position. When their move is safely complete, Red 7 calls the second 'Go' indicating that 8 and 9 can now move. The move is signalled complete by Red 9 calling the smoke off. This tells Red 1 that it is now safe to manoeuvre the new formation shape.

It is essential for every move that the acknowledgement calls come in the correct sequence. This is the safety break and if there is an incorrect call or acknowledgement then everything just stops and nobody moves. The leader can then deal with the situation.

FLYING THE SHOW – THE SECOND HALF

At the end of the first half the formation splits into separate sections. Reds 2–5 remain with the Boss under the callsign 'Enid' (the Famous Five), while Reds 6–9 split off as 'Gypo'. During the second half Enid will perform a series of dynamic five-ship manoeuvres while the Synchro Pair, Reds 6 and 7, commence their series of opposition manoeuvres, and 8 and 9 bat and ball between the two sections performing some manoeuvres with Enid and some with Synchro.

Reds 6 and 7, the Synchro Pair, practise their Mirror formation, with Red 6 flying inverted above Red 7. This forms part of the Corkscrew formation in which Reds 8 and 9, the remaining two members of Gypo, perform barrel rolls behind the Synchro Pair, corkscrewing around their smoke.

Opposite: The Synchro Pair go head-to-head, or 'face up' as they call it, in the inverted during the Opposition Loop. During this manoeuvre they actually 'face up' three times – at the bottom as they pull into the loop, at the top of the loop as seen here, and finally at the bottom of the loop. Note how round and symmetrical that loop is. On calm days like this, if both jets use the same power and speed and pull the same g, it will be totally symmetrical. But if there is a bit of wind, the Synchro Pair have to modify their respective inputs to allow for it and keep their loop even.

Red 8 and Red 9 Goose Reds 1, 2, 3, 4 and 5 on a blustery day at North Weald. A strong wind causes problems for the team leader, who has to work hard to keep the display centred on the datum point.

The Synchro Pair fly the most demanding solo manoeuvres within the display. Although flying at 360 knots, they rarely pull more than 6g (and even then only for short periods). However, the repeated sequence of rapid rolling followed by the very quick application and release of g-force is extremely demanding on both the pilots and the airframes. At the same time as flying individual aerobatic manoeuvres down to 100ft, they have to coordinate with each other to get the passes in the centre of the crowd, and make each one look like they only just miss while flying towards each other at a closing speed of around 800 miles per hour.

It is Red 6's job (Synchro Leader) to get the passes in the centre while Red 7 has to engineer the correct miss-distance to make it look right from the ground. While the miss-distance is only 100ft, there is also a slight correction to account for the crowd's line of sight from the ground. Because they are looking up at the jets, the jet furthest away flies slightly higher so that both aircraft appear to be at the same height; this is called 'fudging'. Synchro achieve their positioning by flying accurate ground patterns which Red 6 assesses in the air and makes corrections to as required during the display.

Although formation flying skills are still relevant to all the pilots in the second half, this part of the show primarily consists of a series of stand-alone manoeuvres. Apart from the flying skill required for the individual manoeuvres, the most difficult aspect of the second half is the coordination between Red 1 and Synchro Leader to ensure that there is always something happening in front of the crowd with no gaps in between. Imagine the situation: you have Synchro performing their opposition passes, Enid performing five-ship manoeuvres, and 8 and 9 flying around, sometimes at speeds in excess of 500 miles per hour, to rejoin another section before their next manoeuvre. And while flying his own jet and leading the Enid manoeuvres, Red 1 is also looking after the overall coordination of all this. Once again, the key is positioning via accurate ground patterns. Reds 1 and 6 reposition between their manoeuvres by flying headings for an exact number of seconds before turning back in towards the crowd. Any errors are assessed instantaneously and a correction made to the ground pattern for the next manoeuvre. It's not rocket science and the concept is straightforward. However, the reality can, at times, be extremely demanding.

PROBLEMS

All of the above describes the skills required to fly the ideal show. On the day, of course, it may be a small crowd, which is very difficult to see from the air, particularly in bad weather. There may be an aircraft problem during the show, perhaps a birdstrike. Or, not unusually in the UK, there may just be a very strong wind affecting all the timings. Well, the key to success is focused training and attention to detail. Show sites are examined by map and photograph before the display. By the start of the season Red 1 can fly the ground patterns so accurately that he can find his way back to even the smallest site in any weather. Aircraft emergencies are discussed constantly throughout the training period so that everybody is aware of the procedures for just about every conceivable occurrence.

Wind is definitely the factor most likely to cause problems on a routine basis. In the display briefing the forecast wind is discussed; on the approach to the site Red 10 will transmit his estimate of the wind from the ground; and during the first half Red 1 will make an airborne assessment of the wind. Then in the second half all ground patterns are wind-corrected and it is even possible to correct errors caused by an incorrect assessment of the wind!

So, in spite of the complexity of a display, the team is well equipped to deliver an outstanding performance, no matter what the circumstances.

CHAPTER 4
Air Shows

THE PLANNING

Every year the Red Arrows receive hundreds of requests from show organisers to perform displays or fly-pasts at their events. The venues range from major international air shows to minor local events. Each October work starts to thrash out the team's programme for the coming display season. Before Christmas the team leader confers with the service's Director of Corporate Communications (i.e. public relations), its Directorate of Recruitment and its Participation Committee (the body which allocates RAF aircraft, equipment and personnel to meet requests for participation in public shows) to consider priorities for the coming year.

Another body that might have an input at this stage is the Defence Export Sales Organisation, which suggests ways in which the Red Arrows might help promote United Kingdom industry abroad. Often the team ends its display season with a foreign tour. Apart from promoting the country, the team's demonstration of the Hawk's capabilities helps boost trade. In such cases the cost of a foreign tour will be borne primarily by the companies involved, which combine their efforts to sponsor the Red Arrows' presence.

The purpose of that early planning meeting is to arrange the various requests in order of priority. As in the case of the earliest RAF displays, the main purposes of the Red Arrows' performances are to promote the RAF in the public eye and to aid service recruitment. Events are chosen with those requirements in mind, though other considerations might also carry weight. An example of the latter might be the decision to send the Red Arrows to display at an event close to one of the RAF's low-flying areas. People in those areas have to live with the noise and disturbance of jet aircraft passing low overhead, and often a Red Arrows display might be used as a 'thank you' for putting up with the inconvenience.

The members of the Participation Committee leave the planning meeting with a list of possible shows for the coming year, from which they construct an initial draft programme. Shows are categorised depending on their perceived value to the service. A high category show is a large, high visibility show in the United Kingdom, such as the Farnborough Air Show or the major displays at Fairford, Southend or Waddington. A medium category show is a large or important show that the team will attend if the date does not clash with an event of higher priority. A lower category show is one of lower priority to service or national interests, which could fit into the Red Arrows' programme provided the team is able to attend.

In January each year the draft programme is established and representatives of the Participa-

Concorde seen from the leader's jet, trailing the supersonic airliner during the rehearsal on 29 May 2002 for the fly-past to celebrate the queen's Golden Jubilee. In this case the runway at RAF Marham played the part of the Mall. This shot was created using a 16mm wide-angle lens, which makes things seem a lot further apart than they really are. In reality, Spike Jepson and I had a face full of Concorde. Dramatic stuff indeed.

Far right: The Red Arrows fly down the Mall in formation with Concorde on 4 June 2002 for the Golden Jubilee fly-past. I was in Red 8, out on the right-hand side. Working out of Stansted on that day, the team was to have taken off at 17:09 hours for a 17:55 fly-past. When we were strapped in and ready to start engines, a call came to delay the take-off. We finally launched about half-an-hour later, and made the run-in down the Mall at around 18:30 hours.

tion Committee visit Scampton to discuss the summer ahead with the team's executive officers. A more refined draft programme is then produced, and Red 10 begins work to establish which of the requested display venues are practicable. At venues where the team has not displayed within the past five years, or at all, a site survey is conducted to check its suitability and identify any potential flight safety problems.

Having established the draft programme, detailed planning begins. The team leader and Red 10 confer with the team pilot designated as navigation officer, to decide which shows can be mounted from Scampton and which ones require the unit to move to an operating base nearer the venue. They also decide where the team will land to refuel, or make overnight stops. Once these

In 1997 the team travelled to Sion in Switzerland to put on a display. The mountainous terrain around Sion necessitated a few alterations to the sequence, and the pre-flight briefing took on a special significance. However, the upturned faces and fingers in ears suggest that at that moment something flying low and fast was drowning out Squadron Leader Simon Meade's words.

factors are agreed, the Junior Engineering Officer decides where and when he will need to position his personnel and ground support equipment.

Once the venues have been finalised as far as possible, the organisers' requested times for each display are considered. At many air shows the organisers like to have the Red Arrows' display as the finale to their event. The Red Arrows are resourceful people, but even they cannot be in two places at the same time. If the organisers of two separate shows request their displays to be flown at the same time, compromise is necessary.

A good example of a compromise was when the air shows at Farnborough and Sunderland in 2002 were held on the same weekend at opposite ends of the country. Both shows are large two-day events accorded high priority. The former is a high-profile international trade show, while the latter attracts huge crowds and provides valuable publicity for the RAF in the

Simon Meade makes some last-minute briefing notes on his pitch map, assisted by Sean Perrett, in preparation for the Mildenhall air show.

Gary Waterfall's mirror sunglasses reflect the action around him, as he and fellow Red Arrows pilots are briefed for the Mildenhall show.

No, it's not a fancy dress party – we really are members of the Red Arrows, honestly! Frazer Wood attempts to explain away strange happenings on Weymouth beach while Iain McIvor tries to pretend he is not there. Meanwhile Steve Underwood, alias Red 10, gives the team leader the latest information on the display site.

'Parky' Parkinson gets down to some serious pre-flight planning at the team's base at Scampton. Usually three of the team's pilots are made responsible for all the navigation planning.

FLT LT CHRISTIAN GLEAVE
CPL STEVE REECE

north-east of England. In each case the organisers wanted the Red Arrows' display to close their respective shows. Obviously that was impossible, so a compromise was worked out. On the Saturday the team's display opened the Farnborough show. Then its planes refuelled and sped north to Sunderland, and gave their performance at the close of the show there. The team and the groundcrews spent the night at Sunderland, and opened the show there on the Sunday. After refuelling, the Hawks flew south and closed the show at Farnborough.

By March each year the team's programme will be almost complete, though some changes might still be needed. At this time the navigation officer begins detailed planning regarding navigation, timing and fuel usage during the transit flights to and from each display. If the display venue happens also to be the airfield from which the team will launch, little navigation planning is

The Red Arrows' day is planned to the second. Here Flight Lieutenant (now Squadron Leader) Christian Gleave checks his watch ready for the check-in.

As the sun beats the retreat at RAF Fairford in Gloucestershire, Corporal Jim Donaldson puts the final polish to a Hawk's canopy. The Red Arrows often close the show at this and other air shows. Organisers request this, reasoning that people will stay to the end to see the Red Arrows perform. For the groundcrew, though, a late display means a late finish to what has probably been a long day.

required. More often, the team needs to transit into the display site, in which case the approach route and timing need to be carefully planned. If, for example, the Red Arrows are due to display at 13:00 hours, a 17 minute 20 second transit from the launching airfield to the display venue means that the team needs to get airborne at 12:42:40 hours. The transit to the venue is not flown in a straight line. Instead, the route includes at least one corner, or dogleg, which the

team leader can cut off should he find it necessary to make up time for any reason.

When all the planning is complete, each week a 'WHAM' is produced for the coming weekend. This gives precise details of timings and movements, ground and air, during each series of displays. This document was first produced many years ago by a road manager who got tired of being continually asked 'What's happening, Manager?'. So he produced a timetable which he

At the Fairford air display, Synchro Lead checks his watch.

Most of the Red Arrows' transit flights over the United Kingdom are made at low level to avoid controlled airspace. Normally the aircraft cruise at 360 knots, or 6 nautical miles per minute. During transit flights the team is usually split into two elements, with Enid section's five aircraft in front and Gypo section's four bringing up the rear. If they happen to pass near an active airfield, the team will give a brief burst of smoke to advertise their presence.

69

Cool dude! Squadron Leader Christian Gleave flies in the Red 9 slot for the 2003 season, his final season with the team. Before he was selected for the team, Gleavie flew Harriers from RAF Laarbruch in Germany and then Hawks as a tactics and weapons instructor at RAF Valley.

circulated to all relevant parties to answer their scheduling questions. The 'WHAM' is now an invaluable device to help ensure that the Red Arrows get to the right place exactly on time.

ON THE DAY

So with all the timings confirmed, the team will set out from Scampton for each sequence of displays.

During transit flights the team leader does the navigation and commands the formation using UHF radio. Traditional map-reading is the basis of his navigation, but there is powerful assistance in the form of the global positioning system (GPS). Each aircraft carries a moving map GPS display, an important aid to accurate timing. The team's navigation officer, flying one of the other Hawks, maintains contact with air traffic control using VHF radio.

In the United Kingdom most transit flights are flown at 1,000ft. The reason for flying at that low altitude is to

Gypo section in transit to RAF Kinloss in Scotland. Red 6 leads the 'finger four' formation with Red 8 to his right and Reds 7 and 9 to his left.

'I see no ships!' Having shut down at RAF Kinloss, before leaving his aircraft 'Gleavie' Gleave surveys the weather.

The rear four jets, Reds 6, 7, 8 and 9, lift off in formation from the runway at Kinloss. Red 6 leads, with Reds 8 and 9 on his right and left respectively. Nearest the camera, in echelon off Red 8, is Red 7.

On arrival at Kinloss the Red
Arrows fly down the runway in Big
Battle formation as the leader
pulls up abruptly before executing
a snappy 7g break. The other
team members follow at two-
second intervals, which
establishes the required spacing
for landing.

72

After landing, the jets' post-flight servicing certificates are filled out, in this case by Sergeant 'Deano' Richmond.

avoid the necessity of trying to get a formation of ten aircraft up and down through cloud. It also avoids most controlled airspace. The 1,000ft altitude is chosen as a compromise to minimise the disturbance of low flying while avoiding most general aviation traffic in the 1,500–3,000ft bracket. It has the added advantages of allowing the team to avoid bad weather and affords exposure to a wider audience than at the display site alone. Such transits are usually made at 360 knots, or 6 miles per minute, though if he needs to make up time the leader can increase speed to as much as 450 knots.

However, flying at 1,000ft is not very economical. Jet engines give their best fuel economy at high altitude. For that reason long-distance transit flights over the United Kingdom and most overseas transit flights are flown at high level using designated airways. On a typical high-level transit the team flies at between 35,000 and 42,000ft, as required by air traffic control, cruising at .7 Mach (420 knots).

Once at the show venue, Red 10 is the leader's eyes and ears. He and the team's video-recorder operator usually arrive by helicopter at least an hour and a half before the display is due to start. Red 10 is in contact with the team leader by mobile phone or radio, depending on whether the team is airborne or not. His first task is to perform a safety sweep of the venue, to look for anything that might constitute a flight safety hazard. This is particularly important at displays that are not centred on airfields, where he will be on the look-out for such things as flocks of birds, activity by microlight aircraft or paragliders, even the odd drifting balloon. He will also check that the organiser's selected datum point for the display remains valid.

As the team approaches the display venue, Red 10 passes details of the weather conditions to the leader by radio. In addition, during the run-in, if the leader needs to establish the exact level of the

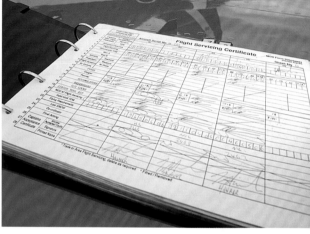

Most overseas transit flights are performed at high level, using designated airways. For this transit to Nancy in France we flew at 42,000ft. In the foreground are Reds 6, 7 and 8 while Enid form their own little package of five jets in the distance. The formation is loose for there's little point in tight, tiring, station keeping when no one is around to see it.

Up at FL420 the air is incredibly clear and the sky registers as a deep blue, against which the jets stand out beautifully.

The air show at RAF Fairford is notoriously difficult to get to by road, with horror stories of queues lasting up to five hours. To avoid this problem the Red Arrows use a helicopter to transport personnel and equipment to the airfield. Here the team leader finishes his Granny Smith apple, before climbing aboard for the short hop from Cheltenham to Fairford.

Helicopter transport is also essential for Red 10, the road manager, to get to many of the venues. He is also the team's safety officer, and has to be present on site whenever the Red Arrows give their display. The helicopter becomes especially useful if the team is doing two displays in a day at venues some distance apart. Here the manager is approaching Southend Airport, cross-referring the datum point against that marked on his site photo.

cloud base, he might order one of the pilots to climb to that level and report back before rejoining the formation. At the display site, depending on the weather, the team flies one of three types of display: full, flat or rolling.

As discussed in Chapter 2, 6,500ft and 2,500ft are the critical cloud-base heights for rolling and full manoeuvres. However, the Red Arrows' display is designed to be flexible. If the weather closes in during the display, the leader might need to order the team to switch between routines.

Alternatively, if the team is engaged in a flat show and the leader sees a patch of clear sky above him, he can order a looping manoeuvre to exploit that change.

Once the display begins, Red 10 has the important task of delivering the commentary over the public address system. He aims to keep the crowd's attention focused to the left, to the right or in front, where it needs to be to appreciate the display fully. At the same time he keeps a wary eye open for any emerging safety problem, such

A rather topsy-turvy view of the world, courtesy of Red 5 and the Revolver. This manoeuvre is used during the rolling and flat displays, when there is a low cloud base. In Cyprus it has to be practised in good weather, like the other manoeuvres. The Revolver is surprisingly difficult to do. The planes are much closer than they appear in this wide-angle view, and the rapid roll to the inverted position can easily cause a pilot to wander.

as an aircraft approaching the site despite the airspace reservation, which the team leader might not have seen. Red 10 is also best placed to point out any faults with the display. If, for example, he sees that one of the pilots has failed to turn off his smoke at the right time, a quick radio call of 'Red 6 [or whoever] Check Smoke' usually puts matters right. At the display venue Red 10 is often the only red-suited pilot the crowd sees. He is therefore the public face of the Red Arrows and he needs to be both approachable and willing to sign a lot of autographs, often at the same time as running back to the helicopter to catch up with Reds 1–9 for the next show.

This detailed procedure for planning and flying each show happens around a hundred times every year, and that's not including all the extra transits between operating bases, sometimes separated by thousands of miles. It is a well-oiled machine, but it needs to be!

As well as being the team's safety officer, Red 10 provides the commentary at each air show. As the team whooshes by in the Wineglass Bend, he keeps the Biggin Hill crowds informed of what is happening and where to look. He also listens on the radio to the team leader's commands, and at an appropriate moment he can relay these over the public address system. The commentary is an important part of the Red Arrows' display, and it greatly enhances the public's enjoyment and understanding of what is happening.

Far left: 'Ladies and Gentlemen, without further ado, it is my pleasure to present the Royal Air Force Aerobatic Team, the Red Arrows!' At sunny Sidmouth the team swoops in from the right for their opening formation, the Big Vixen. The team performed here before a packed sea-front crowd in superb weather. The audience was particularly appreciative, with spontaneous applause greeting the team's arrival and several of the manoeuvres. If you think the pilots cannot hear that applause, you're wrong. Sometimes the road manager keys the microphone of his hand-held radio, so the team members know that their efforts are well received.

The Gleavie and Parky show! The Red Arrows are a close-knit community, and its members spend a lot of time working and socialising together during the display season. The lighter side of life is important, as demonstrated here by Squadron Leader Gleave and Flight Lieutenant Parkinson.

Flight Lieutenant Steve Underwood, Red 10, looking uncharacteristically happy while being photographed. Steve has had a remarkable flying career. Initially he trained as a helicopter pilot, and logged more than 2,000 flying hours in Puma, Wessex and Huey helicopters. In 1989 he became an instructor on Jet Provosts, then he flew Harriers with 1 Squadron at RAF Wittering. Now he has landed what is arguably one of the best of the Red Arrows' jobs. He gets plenty of flying in Hawks and helicopters. At air shows he is usually the only Red Arrows pilot around to receive the appreciation and plaudits from the public. On second thoughts, no wonder he's smiling!

It can be a tough life on the road. Road manager Flight Lieutenant Steve Underwood, video man Corporal Iain 'Mac' McIvor and helicopter pilot Flight Lieutenant John 'JJ' Jackson enjoy lunch at the Southend air show. Sometimes the hospitality is not as good as this, however, leaving the on-site guys to make do with a sandwich or a burger, gobbled down as and when time allows.

Between sorties the Hawks are refuelled and the smoke system's tanks refilled with diesel oil and industrial dyes. Then the cockpit is set up ready for the pilot to climb aboard.

The pilot returns the thumbs-up from his groundcrew. The latter's job is now done and he will walk into position to marshal the jet out of the pan. Unlike the pilots, who are locked in to a maximum tour with the team of three years, groundcrew members can serve for longer or shorter periods.

The longer scheduled inspections of the Hawks take place during the winter off-season, between December and February. However, many of the Red Arrows' jets are now getting old – some were among the original batch issued to the team in 1980 – and it requires a lot of work to keep them in tip-top condition for air shows. If insufficient red-painted Hawks are available for pre-show training, the unit borrows standard aircraft from one of the training schools.

The starboard undercarriage is jacked up while the wheel and tyre are changed. Good serviceability of the Red Arrows' Hawks is vital during both the pre-season training period and the display season. Longer inspections take place during each winter, and are completed in time for the Cyprus detachment. Usually the team takes eleven jets to the island, giving two spares.

The more observant will notice that this formation consists of ten jets rather than the usual nine. That is because the tenth Red Arrow, Red 10, has joined the formation. When operating away from Scampton Red 10 often transits with the team. This enables him to get to the forward operating base quickly, and provides a spare Hawk in case one of the others goes unserviceable.

At the end of a long, two-display day, there is nothing better than a swift pint to help one unwind before a shower, a change and dinner. Red 10 regales the boys with stories of daring do . . .

. . . while Myles, Synchro Lead for 2003, in the best traditions of fighter pilot bar talk, resorts to shooting down his hands.

As for the team leader, perhaps he's wondering what he's let himself in for!

The handling qualities of the Hawks in the Red Arrows' fleet vary from plane to plane. Many of the Hawks are more than twenty years old and have had a hard life. Almost every plane has its own foibles, which make it fly slightly differently from the others. Therefore during the display season each pilot usually flies the same jet with his name painted on the side.

The diesel and dyes for the smoke system are housed in the streamlined tank beneath the belly of the Hawk. Originally designed to house a 30mm Aden cannon, the pods were specially converted for use by the team. Inside the pod are three tanks. The largest, of 50 gallons' capacity, carries neat diesel oil to produce white smoke. The other two tanks, each of 10 gallons' capacity, contain a mixture of diesel oil and blue or red dye to produce trails in those colours. The smoke system devours 10 gallons of liquid per minute, equating to five minutes' duration for white smoke and one minute each for the red and the blue.

The view from Red 4 as it heads into the vertical in the Caterpillar, a manoeuvre which involves looping in trail behind the leader. The white smoke is created by injecting diesel oil into the hot jet efflux, where it is immediately vaporised. To produce the red or blue smoke, industrial dye is added to the diesel oil.

90

This picture of Red 4's rear end shows the three small pipes, one for each colour, that inject the diesel oil and dye into the hot jet efflux to produce the spectacular smoke trails. Switches on the pilot's control column trigger the smoke system, and the appropriate light in the cockpit indicates the colour of smoke selected.

On a cold winter morning at
Cranwell, this Hawk's smoke system
is replenished with diesel oil and
industrial dye.

A Hawk gets remedial attention to its smoke system, while operating out of Exeter airport. The silver suit is worn to safeguard against the terrible staining qualities of the industrial dyes used to produce the red and blue smoke.

The Red Arrows, 2002. From left to right: Red 8, Squadron Leader Chris Carder; Red 6, Squadron Leader Jason 'Jas' Hawker; Red 4, Flight Lieutenant Anthony 'Parky' Parkinson; Red 2, Flight Lieutenant Dave 'DT' Thomas; Red 1, Squadron Leader Carl 'Spike' Jepson; Red 3, Flight Lieutenant John 'JG' Green; Red 5, Squadron Leader Christian 'Gleavie' Gleave; Red 7, Squadron Leader Myles Garland and Red 9, Flight Lieutenant Justin Hughes.

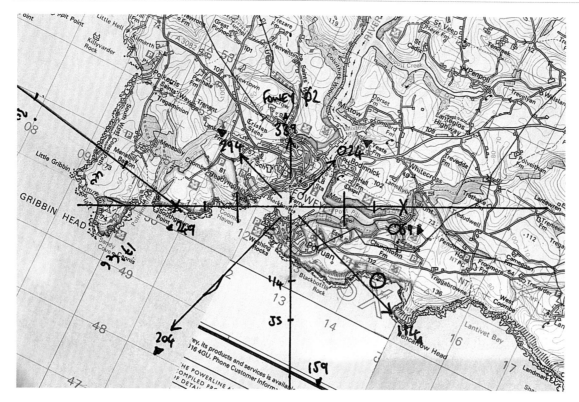

Above: A detail of the pitch map, a 1:50,000-scale Ordnance Survey map showing the axis used for the team's display at Fowey in Cornwall. The central horizontal line runs along the estuary. At 249 degrees is the display line. The datum point, on which the display is centred, is where that line intersects the opposing vertical, the 339 degrees 'crowd front 90 degree' line.

Right: After the Fowey display the Red Arrows land at Exeter Airport. Usually the pilots don't get to meet the crowds, but the Fowey display is different. By tradition, the team is invited there afterwards by the townsfolk and receive a rapturous welcome. Team members then take part in the annual Pasty Ceremony, helping to carry a huge Cornish pasty for consumption by the local children. It is a memorable experience – ask Jas Hawker.

Far right: At Fowey in 2002 Chris Carder goes head-to-head with Enid section, at a combined closing speed of around 800 knots. Having flown through the inverted 'v', he then pulls up through their wake in the Goose. Fowey is one of the team's favourite venues. As well as being very scenic, the hilly terrain makes it challenging. This picture was taken from the castle at Coombe Haven.

Nowadays it is rare for the Red Arrows to operate from the base at which they display, the Mildenhall air show being an exception. When the team's Hawks are parked near the crowd, the start-up and shut-down procedures are executed formally and in unison, in keeping with the team's polished image. Once the technicians have readied their jets, they line up in front of them.

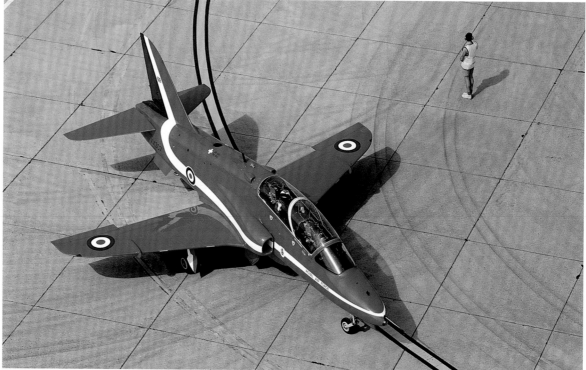

A Hawk follows the yellow line to the runway. As each jet leaves the pan it passes between two technicians, who give it one final visual check. In particular they look for fluid leaks or loose panels, and make sure that the pins for each ejector seat and the explosive cord have been removed and are visible in their proper housings.

Before he briefs the team for a particular display, the leader studies the weather forecast for the route and the venue. With that information he can decide whether to run the full, flat or rolling display. In the description that follows Spike Jepson takes us through a full display taking place over the launching airfield, with no weather or other complications.

By the time we conduct our formal pre-display brief, I will have thought through most potential problems. We like to run that briefing as short a time as possible before we strap in. Typically, from finishing the briefing to checking in on the radio will be about five minutes. That way we remain totally focused and minimise unwelcome distractions. Preparation, anticipation and timing are everything for us. We run our display to the second, and of necessity it has to be a very slick operation.

Once we have completed our briefing, we walk straight to the jets and strap in. The radio check is at the appointed time. I call 'Reds Check' and everybody checks in, rapidly: '2, 3, 4, 5, 6, 7, 8, 9.' We then do the same with each aircraft's second radio.

Flight Lieutenant Dicky Patounas gets the thumbs-up – it's 'all systems go' on a particularly windy day in 2000.

The Hawk's tyres kick up moisture from a wet Kinloss taxiway.

Next, I say 'Reds with 1150, start up, go', the 1150 referring to the amount of fuel in kilograms which each aircraft should have. We start shows with different fuel weights depending on the location of the nearest diversion and this is an important reminder for the pilots to check they have the correct amount of fuel. It takes three minutes from the radio check-in until the Hawks have started their engines and are ready to taxi.

At some display venues the Red Arrows' Hawks are parked in a line in full view of the crowd. In such instances the formal display begins when the nine groundcrew march out to their jets. Each man halts in front of his aircraft, and turns to face the crowd, standing to attention. When the pilots arrive and climb into their cockpits, the technicians help them strap in. They then return to their positions in front of their aircraft, again standing to attention. Once the pilots have checked-in on the radios and are ready to start the engines, they close their canopies in turn. The technicians then turn to face their aircraft, each holding a fire extinguisher, ready to watch over the engine start. The team leader orders the pilots to start engines, which they do in unison. Then the pilots check the operation of their flight controls, flaps and airbrakes. They do this in unison, so the move looks smart and coordinated.

Sometimes during the start-up procedure a pilot might discover that his aircraft has a technical problem. If the groundcrew cannot fix it immediately, the pilot will unstrap and run to the spare aircraft and strap into that one. Spike Jepson again:

The Red Arrows fly by in Big Vixen, one of the most pleasing of their formation shapes.

The team hits the vertical in the Kite then, as they pull over the top of the loop, they change into Apollo formation.

Once the engines are started, I check-in on the ground frequency to find out the runway in use, the airfield pressure and the wind speed and direction. We taxi out in numerical order, short spaced to avoid taking up too much room on the taxiway. On leaving the parking area the Hawks proceed in single file past two technicians, one on either side, for the 'last chance' checks. In particular they check that our ejection-seat pins are out and stowed, and the flaps are set for take-off. Those two things could definitely kill you if they are not done correctly. The technicians also check that all panel fasteners and the smoke pods are secure, and there is no sign of leaking fluid. As each plane passes the check, each technician gives a 'thumbs-up'.

The Hawks taxi out and as the last pilot leaves the parking area he calls 'all aboard'. As the leader nears the runway threshold, he requests permission from the tower for the team to enter the runway and line up. Once clearance is received, the jets taxi on to the runway. In this case they will go straight into their display, so they will split into three sections on the runway. Typically the leader, Red 2 and Red 3 move to a point 1,500ft down the runway. Red 4 and Red 5 stop 750ft behind them, on the right and left of the runway respectively. Reds 6, 7, 8 and 9 halt 750ft further back, at the runway threshold.

One minute before our scheduled take-off time, I will call for take-off clearance. Once this is received, I confirm the type of take-off we will do. If we are going straight into the display I will call 'Display Take-Off, Coming Left'. Red 6, who leads the rear four, will acknowledge this. With 30 seconds to go I repeat the type of take-off and then call 'Smoke, Lights On, Go, Power, Parking Brakes'. 'Smoke' is a reminder to check that the smoke system is turned on. 'Lights' means we turn on the nose lights, together. 'Power' means that everyone opens the throttles together and checks their engine instruments. 'Parking Brakes' tells each pilot to make sure his parking brake is off before he begins his take-off roll – it would be highly embarrassing if someone forgot to do that!

I then call 'Reds, Rolling, Now'. On the 'Now' we let off the brakes and start to accelerate down the runway. A quick glance in my mirrors confirms that Red 2 and Red 3 are with me, tucked in close. As we pass through 140 knots I ease back gently on the stick, and the nose and main wheels lift off the ground.

Once airborne I select the undercarriage up, then the flaps. Then I gently throttle back from 97 per cent to 93 per cent power. A glance in my mirrors should show Red 4 and Red 5 closing in, flying slightly high to avoid my jetwash. Meanwhile, at the back end Red 6 will be leading the other three in their take-off. Once airborne, they form into box formation and close on me rapidly. I commence a very gentle turn to the left, so Red 6 can bring his four planes in to complete our Diamond Nine formation. When he is in place he calls 'Aboard', to let me know. I then call 'Smoke Off, Go'.

The team now turns through 180 degrees to a position behind the crowd. The leader calls 'Nine Arrow, Go', and Red 8 and Red 9 acknowledge to confirm they are moving into position. Next comes the Big Vixen formation, followed by the Kite formation. Safety is of paramount importance during the display, and Spike outlines some of the precautions taken:

We have a prepared sequence of calls that puts a safety break in anything we do. So when I call 'Kite, Go' that is acknowledged by Red 6 and Red 7. When Red 7 is in position he calls 'Go', which Red 8 and Red 9 acknowledge. Once the latter has acknowledged, they both move. If anyone fails to acknowledge a call, it means either that he has a technical problem or has suffered a radio failure. In that unlikely event, the display sequence is halted and nobody moves until the situation has been resolved.

In Kite formation we enter a loop and midway up the loop I call 'Apollo, Go', and we move into Apollo formation. Red 8 and Red 9 acknowledge the move, followed by Reds 6, 4 and 5. Reds 6, 8 and 9 move forward into position, while Reds 4 and 5 slide back to complete the Apollo formation. As I go over the top of the loop, I look back at the display line. That helps me judge the pull-out, and I twist the formation so that it arrives at the datum point flying at 300ft above the ground.

Every so often I take a picture that really stands out from the rest. This, for me, is one such image. It was taken during the first part of the Jubilee Split, when Reds 2, 3, 4 and 5 fanned out from the leader who then continues to loop with Gypo section in trail. We are looking from Red 1 as Red 3 and Red 5 rudder away. The horizon, in the distance, is slightly tilted, but that does not matter. The important thing, for this picture, was to get the jets placed symmetrically in the frame as they split. But the factors that really made this picture for me are the low-key lighting and the effervescent white smoke against the blue backdrop.

One scene that, from the cockpit, never fails to grab one's attention is the Goose. Reds 2, 3, 4 and 5 step down in an inverted 'v' beneath the leader while Red 8, Squadron Leader Chris Carder, flies through the gap in the middle. We were doing about 300 knots while Chris was going flat out at about 500 knots. That gave a combined closing speed of 800 knots. Because of the difference in speeds, Red 8's main problem is to get the timing right so that the cross-over happens over the datum point, the crowd centre.

The shadows reveal Enid section, Reds 1 to 5, to be in vic formation, setting up for the Goose as they overfly Scampton's taxiway.

One of the favourites for the crowd is the Heart. It is created by Red 6 and Red 7, followed by Red 9 who provides the arrow. Usually it is performed using white smoke, which shows up beautifully against a blue sky. However, if there is a blanket of cloud the amorous three use red smoke instead. The Heart is frequently dedicated to someone in the crowd, often a friend or relative of one of the pilots. Red 10, being an upstanding chap, resists bribery in the selection process – or so we're told!

As the Hawks curve round in front of the crowd, they move into Wineglass formation. Red 2 and Red 3 then start moving forwards into line abreast, to the right and left of the leader respectively:

I now have two guys flying close on either side of me, moving gently around. That can be distracting, so I try to ignore their presence and concentrate on the datum point and establishing the bend. I cannot see Red 8 and Red 9 moving in behind me, so I rely on the latter's call 'Smoke Off, Go', to tell me they have completed their move safely and everyone is in position. I can now manoeuvre the formation as required.

I sweep the Wineglass formation past the datum point in front of the crowd, and at the end of the pass I call 'EFA, Go'. Reds 2 and 3 move back and Reds 4 and 5 move forwards and outwards. As soon as I assess they are safely clear of Red 8 and Red 9, I call for those guys to move into the next position: 'Nine-Arrow, Go'. Red 8 and Red 9 acknowledge, then move into position in echelon outside Red 4 and Red 5, for our widest formation.

The leader now prepares for a formation roll, for which he needs to use exactly the right amount of bank and to pull exactly the right amount of g-force. Probably one of the most difficult tasks facing the leader is that of keeping the roll consistent throughout its entire revolution.

After the formation roll the leader holds the bank at 30 degrees and flies towards the crowd in

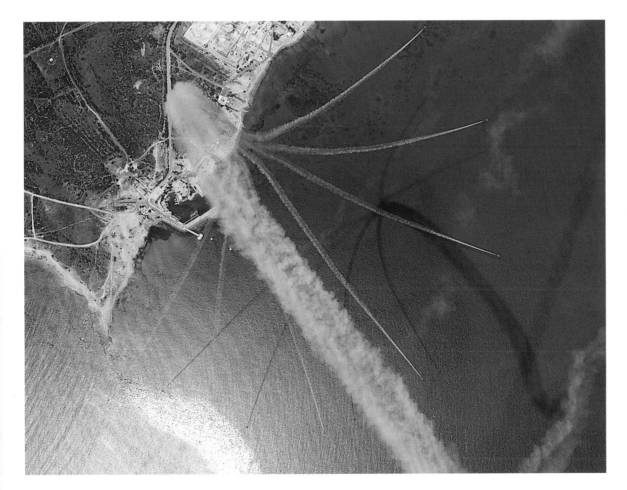

Another lofty view, courtesy of Red 10, as Reds 1, 2, 3, 4 and 5, plus Reds 8 and 9, fan out in the Vertical Break. The jets loop in Vixen formation, then split after passing over the top. On the leader's command each jet, except his own which forms the central spoke, rotates to a briefed angle and then pulls up.

Eagle formation for the Quarter Clover, a loop with a 90-degree roll. The jets then descend steeply, pointing straight at the datum point. Once through the Quarter Clover, the Hawks change into Diamond formation and sweep past the front of the crowd. They then reverse their turn, and move into Concorde formation. There is a smooth, majestic roll in Concorde in front of the crowd, before the team moves into Chevron formation. Next comes the Jubilee Split, the

manoeuvre that takes the team into the second half of the show. Spike explains:

I position the team pointing towards the crowd in Chevron formation. I call 'Smoke on, Go' and pull up into the start of a loop. At 45 degrees nose-up, I call the formation to split and Reds 2–5 gently fan out in the vertical. I continue the loop and at 60 degrees nose-down, I break away from the remaining four aircraft, and they perform their split on the way down.

Reds 1, 2 and 3 pull up into the Caterpillar. In trail, it is important that each aircraft keeps out of the jet efflux from the aircraft in front by flying slightly below it. Hot exhaust gases entering an engine air intake can cause a flame-out.

Opposite: Against a superb deep blue sky, Reds 1, 2, 3, 4 and 5, plus Reds 8 and 9, loop in Vixen formation then fan out in the Vertical Break.

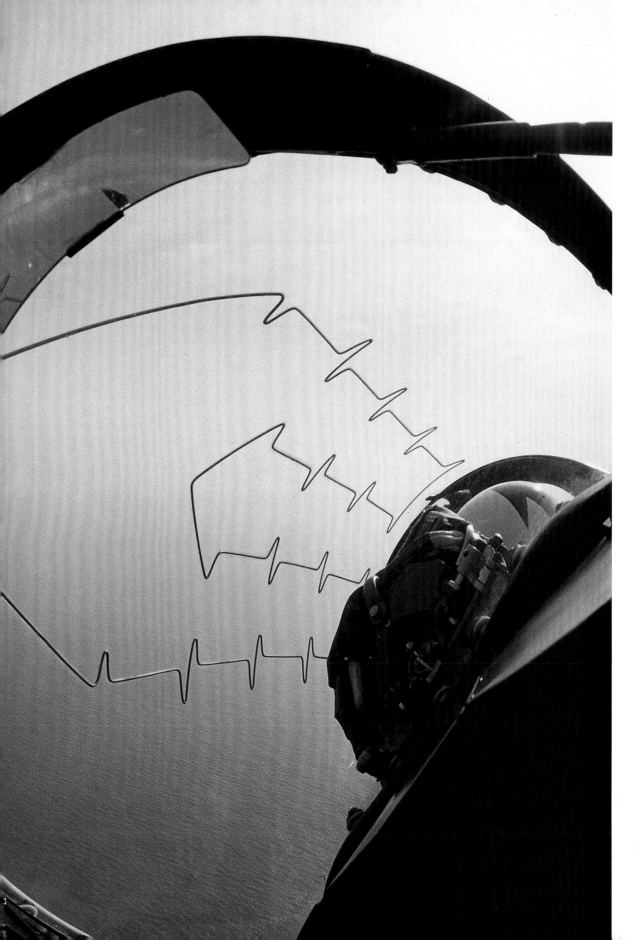

During the second half of the display, Red 5 trails behind his four team-mates as they set up for the Caterpillar. The distance between the jets is greatly enhanced by the use of the 16mm ultra-wide-angle lens.

astern and on to his right-hand side, in preparation for the Twizzle.

> I perform a descending barrel roll with Reds 2, 3, 4 and 5 in trail. The Twizzle manoeuvre is one of the most difficult to get right consistently. After it I call 'Letting It Out, Rolling Out'. I then round the corner with 70 degrees of bank, pulling 2.5g, and head for the datum point. Red 8 and Red 9 now rejoin us, in preparation for the Vixen Break. For this manoeuvre we first run in and loop. For best visual effect, it is essential that I head directly towards the crowd centre. As we go over the top of the loop, the Synchro Pair should be finishing their Opposition Barrel Roll. I call 'Break, Break, Go' and all seven jets fan out flying at their briefed angles and trailing smoke. I pull into a steep climb going straight ahead, to form the central spoke of the fan. When I call 'Smoke Off, Go', that brings the display to an end.

The show might be over, but as he heads away from the datum point the leader needs to reform the team behind him. He lets out a brief burst of smoke to assist the others to see him and rejoin the formation.

During each display the team leader's aim is to fly each manoeuvre smoothly and consistently. He wants to make all normal radio calls, moves and control inputs identical to those used during earlier displays. Only in that way will his pilots know instinctively what is coming, and the control inputs they will need. Such a requirement is easy to state but much more difficult to achieve, however. Spike explained:

> To consistently produce a good show, all my control inputs need to be as predictable as possible. The people flying on my wings need to anticipate every move I make. It is important that they are not being reactive. And the further back in the formation they fly, the more critical that becomes. But I am not a robot, and occasionally my input will be fractionally different from that expected. If I roll a little too fast, or go into a loop with too 'soft' a pull, there will be evidence of it on the show video for all to see. An apparent ripple running through the formation would indicate that I had made a control input that was slightly different from that anticipated, and as a result I had unsettled the guys. When that happens they will let me know about it at the debrief, and in no uncertain terms!

So much for the team leader's views on the display. As we shall see in the next chapter, it all looked very different to the author, sitting in the rear seat of one of the manoeuvring Hawks and trying to photograph the dramatic scenes around him.

CHAPTER 6

Flying in the Hawk

Fast-jet military aviation is a potentially hazardous business, and one that does not suffer fools gladly. For those who do not participate in it regularly, it is also a hostile and unfamiliar environment. The BAE Systems Hawk flown by the Red Arrows is a two-seat advanced trainer and it therefore boasts a complete array of controls within the rear cockpit, including the stick, rudder bars and throttle.

Before an outsider can be considered for a flight with the team, in any capacity, he or she must have been cleared as medically fit. There are tests on the heart, the chest, the abdomen, the spine, the ears and the blood pressure. The potential passenger must also fit within the height and weight criteria of the ejection system, which has minimum and maximum limits.

Assuming the RAF is satisfied that one's mind and body are both capable of withstanding the physical demands of fast-jet aviation, the next step is to be fitted out with a set of flying kit. First there is the flight suit – a green one, I'm afraid, as those highly prized red ones are only for the ten pilots, the two engineering officers and the team manager. Irrespective of their colour, RAF flight suits are made from a fire-retardant material capable of withstanding a direct flame

The team leader's highly recognisable helmet awaits its master. Made largely of Kevlar, it is very light, an important consideration when operating in a high g environment.

for a short period. Footwear comprises a pair of thick socks, with stout flying boots that give ankle protection in case of a parachute descent and rough landing.

Next comes the flying helmet (or 'bone dome') and oxygen mask. Over the years the design of these has improved greatly, and the modern Mk 10B helmet is reasonably comfortable to wear and light in weight. A correctly fitting 'bone dome' is most important, and the unit's safety equipment workers ensure this is the case (an ill-fitting helmet, moving about on the wearer's head, could be dangerous during an ejection). The helmet has two retractable visors made of toughened plastic, one clear and one darkened.

At least one visor has to be in the down position at all times during the flight, to protect the eyes in case of ejection or a birdstrike on the cockpit canopy. As well as delivering oxygen to the wearer, the oxygen mask houses the microphone for communication by radio and with the pilot.

Next comes the 'Mae West' life-jacket, a waistcoat with an inflatable bladder to provide flotation if the wearer comes down in water. The 'Mae West' houses the personal locating beacon,

a radio beacon to enable rescuers to home in on its signal, also a heliograph and a whistle to summon attention.

A pair of white cape leather gloves and a pair of canvas leg restraints to fit around the lower legs complete the ensemble. The leather gloves protect the hands in case of fire or an ejection. The leg restraints are worn on each leg just below the knee, and are fitted with metal rings. During strapping in, webbing straps are passed from the

Far left: Simon Meade, the team leader from 1997 to 1999, discusses a snag on his jet with a member of the groundcrew. In addition to a 'Mae West' life-jacket, Simon wears a g-suit around his legs and abdomen. When the aircraft pulls g, a bladder running down the outside of each leg inflates with compressed air. The tightening effect of this around the legs and abdomen prevents the blood from draining to those parts of the body, and increases the pilot's tolerance to g-forces.

Left: The canopy of one of the Hawks receives a thorough pre-flight polish. It is important that it is clean and provides the pilot (and photographer!) with a clear all-round view. The zig-zag line embedded in the Perspex is an explosive cord, which detonates immediately the ejector seat handle is pulled, shattering the canopy and thus providing a way for the ejection seat and its occupant to pass through.

securing points on the cockpit floor, via the metal rings, into the ejector seat. On ejection, those webbing straps automatically pull the legs against the bottom of the seat and hold them securely in place. This prevents the legs flailing around in the airflow when the seat leaves the aircraft, which could result in serious injuries.

The next step is the briefing on the ejection seat. Before the flight the occupant's weight must be dialled on the seat. This gives optimum ejection seat performance. Once the seat handle is pulled, its operation thereafter is automatic. First, an explosive cord embedded in the Hawk's canopy detonates. That shatters the canopy, providing in an instant a safe path for the seat and its occupant to pass through. The seat leaves

the cockpit within half a second of the handle being pulled. The next thing its occupant knows, he or she is hanging from a fully inflated parachute with the personal survival pack, containing a life-raft and other items of survival equipment, dangling below at the end of a 17ft-long webbing line.

Before they are allowed to fly with the formation, outsiders must undergo a check ride. This g-laden aerobatic sortie familiarises the passenger with the environment, and looks for reasons why the candidate is unfit to fly with the formation. That said, very few civilians are allowed to fly in the display formation. Most journalists have to make do with a sortie in the chase aircraft.

If I fly with the Red Arrows (or in any other fast-jet aircraft), I always plan to have plenty of time to get ready. It would be quite unacceptable for the sortie to be delayed owing to my lateness. I double-check all my gear and then make a final check of my flight kit, to make sure it is all still there, and carry out a final check of my camera kit.

Today I am flying with Red 4, my favourite position in the formation. For most of the time Red 4 flies on the extreme right of the nine-plane formations. Being right-handed, I find it easier to take pictures looking out to the left side of the aircraft where the action is.

On entering the jet, one must first check that the ejection seat handle arming pin is in place, making the seat 'safe'. I also check the inside and the outside of the canopy for greasy marks or smears that could interfere with photography. Next I don my 'Mae West', and check that my spare films are secure in the right-hand pocket of my flight suit. Unused films go in my right pocket, used films in my left. Usually I take six rolls with me during a flight with the Red Arrows. I will have removed each film from its plastic canister beforehand.

Now I am all set, and still with time in hand. Nevertheless I get strapped in early, which gives me the opportunity to relax when it is done. First, the umbilical fitted to the 'Mae West' clips in to the left-hand side of the ejection seat with a reassuring 'clunk'. This will provide me with oxygen and communications. Next, the restraining straps are fed through the leg restraint rings and plugged into the ejection seat. Then I clip the personal survival pack connector to the left side of the seat. In the event of an ejection, this lanyard will automatically switch on the personal locating beacon which starts sending a distress call.

The combined ejection seat and parachute harness is next to be fitted. During a sortie involving inverted flight, it is particularly

During the second half of the show, Reds 1, 2, 3, 4 and 5 (we are in Red 4) play follow-my-leader as we head for the datum point. The leader's job has been likened to 'flying a Jumbo jet-sized fighter through aerobatic manoeuvres'. Rather than pull high g turns, during the formation set-ups his job is to fly each manoeuvre smoothly and consistently. He must also ensure the display is centred on the datum point.

Yet another of my favourites, the fuselage of XX253 beautifully bracketed by cockpits above, below and behind. The telephoto lens helped to compress the distance between the jets. Although they are close, the lens has made them appear one on top of the other. This image is another great example of the results one gets from transparency film. Exposed for the brightly lit jets, the film cannot handle the differential between them and the blue sea background. Although the sea was dark, it was not this dark.

asks if I am ready for the canopy to come down. As soon as the canopy is down and secure, I remove and stow my two arming pins, to make 'live' the ejection system. To confirm this I call 'Two Pins!'

By now 'Parky' has started the Adour engine, and a whiff of the exhaust's acrid smell permeates my oxygen mask. Within a minute or so he has completed the post-engine start checks and we taxi forwards, obeying the hand signals of our crew chief and following Reds 1, 2 and 3. As we are about to clear the parking area one of the engineers gives us a final visual

check as previously described, then confirms all is well with a smart 'thumbs-up'.

On the way to the runway my pilot goes through the Abort Briefing. I have heard it many times before, but each time it focuses my attention on the potential dangers of fast-jet flight. He lists the various emergency scenarios on take-off, and our reactions to each one. On take-off the most profound emergency is an engine failure. Depending on our speed and the length of runway in front of us, he must decide whether to brake hard, run into the barrier or order me to eject. Then he goes through the pre-take-off checks:

Another view of Enid section over the sea off Cyprus. This picture was taken using a 20mm wide-angle lens, which allowed me to get in a lot of the background. The wonderful highlight caught on the calm sea turns an otherwise pedestrian picture into something special.

- Harness secure and locked
- Weight dialled into ejection seat
- Personal survival pack connected
- Command eject lever down
- Two pins stowed
- At least one of the two helmet visors in the 'down' position

By now my heart is racing in anticipation of the take-off run and flight ahead. Today's display is an 'In-Season Practice' or ISP. The team members need to maintain their proficiency during the season and will fly one of these practices whenever there is a five-day period without a public show. As a civilian, I am not permitted to fly with the team during public shows. So for me, the pre-season work-up in

Cyprus is the principal opportunity to conduct air-to-air photography, complemented by the occasional ISP over Scampton.

The weather is good, so it will be the full display. We taxi on to the runway for a display take-off. Reds 1, 2 and 3 are ahead of us in 'vic' formation, Reds 6, 7, 8 and 9 trailing in Finger Four formation. We are in the middle, with the width of the runway separating us from Red 5 opposite. My camera is at the ready, as usually there is a good opportunity to take pictures during take-off.

I am, however, always fully aware of the possibility of disaster during the take-off. A tyre blow-out, a birdstrike or an engine failure might require an instant reaction and I'd need to get rid of my camera quickly, throwing it against the

Another view from the leader's jet, looking over my left shoulder, using a 35–70mm zoom lens set at 35mm. Wearing full flying kit, strapped tightly into the ejection seat and fighting the unrelenting g-forces, taking such photographs is no easy task. The black edging is the canopy sill. Although obtrusive, I think it adds drama to the shot.

blast screen in front of me. I dismiss any heroic notions of taking the camera with me: the huge acceleration forces would wrench it from my hands, perhaps smashing it into and breaking one of my legs. My camera has no strap on it, for two reasons. First, if I had to eject and the strap was round my neck, during the seat's rapid acceleration the strap could break my neck. And secondly, because it might become wrapped around the control column – another undesirable occurrence.

When the jets are all in position on the runway, Red 1 (Spike Jepson) gives the now familiar command 'Smoke. Lights on, Go. Power. Parking brakes', followed by 'Reds, Rolling, Now'. The acceleration down the runway is

Opposite: The leader's Hawk loops off the Akrotiri coastline, with me in the rear seat. For such shots I use a clamped, lightweight, rear-facing camera fitted with a 16mm wide-angle lens.

129

rapid, and in just a few seconds we are airborne. We rapidly overhaul Reds 1, 2 and 3, and move into position to form the right-hand element of the formation. As we bank, the four remaining jets slot into position for the Diamond Nine formation.

Although I have seen this sight many times, I never tire of it. Off to our left are the eight other jets, each one moving up and down, back and forth, within its own small piece of airspace. It never ceases to amaze me how much relative movement there is between the individual jets. From the ground the Red Arrows look as if they are locked on to one another, but from close up one can see the continual jockeying, as each pilot manipulates the throttle and stick to maintain his position in the formation. From my position it is not possible to tell which type of formation we are flying, for the planes look like a mass of seething red and white.

By now, we are into the display proper and I am well on the way through my first roll of film. Slow down, calm down, I say to myself, you don't want to run out! With aerial photography the challenge is to capture the pictures while working around and coping with one's environment. Strapped into an ejection seat and wearing the paraphernalia of flight, it is hard enough to turn through 90 degrees to see the action, let alone try to compose perfect pictures as well.

For reasons of safety, I keep my airborne camera equipment to an absolute minimum. I take one camera body, with new batteries installed unless I know they are good. Once, before a flight in a Jaguar, I omitted to check my camera batteries beforehand. As we taxied out I started taking pictures and the battery symbol flashed: my batteries were low. On that occasion I was lucky and I got away with it, for the battery held out for the flight. But I shall never forget that feeling of impending helplessness –

This is another favourite picture of mine. It was taken in 2000 over the Mediterranean, looking down in a 90-degree bank. From certain angles the sea appears black on film, as here. It does not look that way to the eye, it is just that the slide film I use cannot cope with the exposure differential. Using 100 ASA film, the camera is set at f8 with a shutter speed of 1/320th second, exposing the brightly lit jets correctly, but under-exposing the sea in the background.

From a photographic point of view, angles, lenses, exposures and, most important of all, composition all combine to create a dramatic picture. While flying in the formation, nothing can be preset. Therefore the skill lies in creating different images from the same position during different flights. While this shot is not one of my most dramatic, I love its composition and urgency, with the white smoke trail from the leader's jet making the picture.

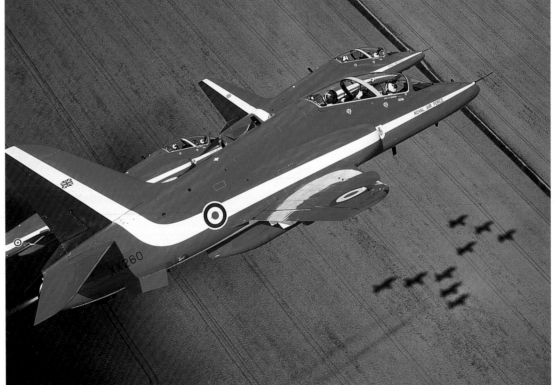

This shot was surprisingly difficult to take. During this long banked turn we were pulling an almost constant 3g, which made my arms and my camera weigh three times more than normal. That might not seem much, but when you have been fighting that level of g for a goodly amount of time you certainly know it! Usually reflections off the canopy will ruin a picture like this. The geometry dictates that when we see our shadow on the ground, it is there for only about four seconds during a 360-degree turn. Precisely at this time the sun, at 90 degrees to the canopy, will often cause terrible white reflections. Looking at the jets gives no indication of the formation they are in but the shadows on the ground reveal they are in Wineglass.

I was on a once-in-a-lifetime flight and at any moment the camera might fail owing to my negligence and laziness. I resolved that such a situation will never, ever, happen again.

Currently I use a Nikon F90 camera fitted with a 35–70mm zoom lens for air-to-air work. The F90 is light, compact and easily gripped, which is a major advantage when one has to combat g-forces. During the first half of the Red Arrows' display, when all nine aircraft move as one, there are a lot of long curves around the datum point, as the team traverses in its various formation shapes. Although the forces are moderate, around 3 or 4g, they are continuous. After even a short time holding one's arms and camera up against this unrelenting, unseen force, my shoulders ache

Rear-facing view from the leader's jet during the Revolver. Spike rolls upside down and holds the inverted position. A couple of seconds later Red 4 and Red 5, on the left and the right, simultaneously roll inverted also. This manoeuvre is used only during the rolling and flat shows.

Photographed looking towards the
sun, the smoke and the shadows
make a dramatic effect.

An important part of the photographer's art is to create unusual images of the available scenes. Composition is everything. When looping and rolling I usually try to square up the horizon, which looks more natural. But, because I am travelling in a jet which is formating on other planes, it is more comfortable to square on the jets and accept an angled background. Although I do this for variation, often I get a stronger image by tilting the camera to square the horizon.

and burn! (Bear in mind that during those long banking turns my arms and my camera weigh three or four times more than normal.)

One of the most frustrating aspects of photography through a jet's cockpit canopy is the reflections that come off the Perspex. These are worst when banking or looking down towards the ground while photographing the jets below. Those reflections are incredibly hard to eliminate, and often they will ruin what would otherwise be a great picture. I use a home-made extended lens hood, which reduces the problem to some extent.

Reloading a camera in the air requires a surprising amount of concentration and effort. A roll of film dropped on the floor of the cockpit becomes a flight safety hazard as it could jam the controls and cause an accident. If a film were to be dropped, the pilot would immediately pull out of the formation. Once at a safe distance he

Although not the most colourful of photographs, this shot screams drama and character. The image was captured during an in-season practice flight from Scampton. I love the way the jets are in shade while the multi-coloured background is a mix of sun and shadow, the latter imitating faithfully the mid-height cumulus cloud that had caused it.

would turn the aircraft upside down in the hope that the renegade film would float up to the top of the canopy from where I could grab it. But if it had slipped into a nook beneath the cockpit flooring, the jet would be grounded until the roll was retrieved. Obviously prevention is much better than cure and I am happy to report that after hundreds of airborne reloads I have never yet dropped a roll of film. This is largely due to taking great care, and not trying to rush the

reloading process. Each movement – removing the used film from the camera and putting it into my left pocket, taking a fresh roll from my right and loading it into the camera – I do very deliberately. But it's not easy – I have to do all that while the aircraft is looping and rolling, and going from positive to negative g!

I am also respectful of the flight controls, particularly the control column, while taking pictures and reloading. On occasions I have

Yet another colourful image of the team set against the dark backdrop of the Mediterranean.

When the jets are going straight up at 90 degrees to the horizon, photography is relatively simple. However, to appreciate my viewpoint, the reader should turn the book clockwise through 90 degrees!

experience I have learned not to attempt to hold up the camera during a 6g turn. Before a hard manoeuvre like the Vixen Break, the safest place for my camera is on top of my knee and held firmly in place with both hands.

A further problem facing the aerial photographer is that for much of the time one has to be looking through the viewfinder of the camera. Imagine the scenario. We begin a formation loop and, as we approach the vertical, a rolling movement is added. Throughout this time I am concentrating on holding my viewfinder on the principal subject – the jets upon which we are formating. My eyes tell me that we are flying straight and level – because the subject on which I am focused seems so to be, relative to us. However, my inner ear and other non-visual senses are crying out 'No we're not, we're looping and rolling!' If one were prone to motion sickness, those are just the conditions to bring it on.

Despite the occasional spell of discomfort, I count myself privileged to experience the world of the Red Arrows. The flying is incredible. And the more one does, the better it gets. It gives me great personal satisfaction to create the photographs that capture those elite aviators in action.

Sean Perrett and Andy Offer stroll in after yet another routine day at the office. Theirs is a tough job, but somebody has to do it!

143

Acknowledgements

In assembling the material for this book I received help from a lot of people. Due to the numbers involved, it is impossible to thank individually everyone who assisted me, but I would like to name those who went that extra mile. If I have forgotten anyone, I sincerely apologise.

My thanks go to the 2002 team, Sqn Ldr Carl 'Spike' Jepson, Flt Lt Dave Thomas, Flt Lt John Green, Flt Lt Tony Parkinson; Sqn Ldr Christian Gleave, Flt Lt Jason Hawker, Sqn Ldr Myles Garland, Sqn Ldr Chris Carder and Flt Lt Justin Hughes. I should also like to thank the tenth 2002 Red Arrow, Flt Lt Steve Underwood, the team's tireless manager. Thanks are also due to Sqn Ldr Lyn Johnson, the Senior Engineering Officer Sqn Ldr Mark Northover and the Junior Engineering Officer Flt Lt Tim Beagle, Wg Cdr Bill Ramsey, Gp Capt Jon Fynes, Sqn Ldr Richard Carleton, WO John May and Flt Lt Howard Leader. Finally, there are the three new pilots selected to join the team for the 2003 season, Flt Lts Jez Griggs, Dunc Mason and Dan Simmons.

I also need to thank the previous team leaders, Wg Cdr Simon Meade and Wg Cdr Andy Offer, plus team members Sqn Ldr Mike Williams, Flt Lt Ian Smith, Sqn Ldr Gary Waterfall; Sqn Ldr Andy Cubin, Flt Lt Tim Couston, Flt Lt Dave Stobie, Flt Lt Richie Matthews, Flt Lt Sean Perrett, Sqn Ldr Dicky Patounas, Flt Lt Andy Evans, Sqn Ldr Andy Lewis, Flt Lt Russ Jones, Sqn Ldr Jim Provost, Sqn Ldr Mark Cutmore, Wg Cdr 'Ginge' Paige, Sqn Ldr Dave Chowns, Sqn Ldr Jon Russell and Sqn Ldr Al McNeil.

I would also like to thank Dr Claire McCready for doing the medicals, Dr Jeremy Gittins for helping me to pass them, and Eric Ward of the Red Arrows Trust.

It would be inappropriate to close without saying a big thank you to the unsung heroes of the team, the 'Blues', together with the behind-the-scenes personnel without whom the Red Arrows could not function. Flt Sgt Tim Latham; Chief Techs Graham Ayres, Dave Densham, Stu Frazer, Marty Morgan; Sgts Dave Ablard, Ian Blake, Gary Cavanagh, Terry Cheadle, Ashleigh Doo, Garry Holt, Steve Hutchinson, Tim Jacklin, Charlie Marr, Glen Parker, Richard Peacock, Mark Ratcliffe, Deano Richmond, Andy Roberts, Doc Savage, Bob Taylor; Cpls Stephen Campbell, Andy Cole, Reg Davies, Jim Donaldson, Mark Dove, Malcolm Faulder, Mark Gage, Nick Green, Stuart Green, Harry Harrison, Mark Jones, Craig Lynch, Kenny McCreadie, Iain McIvor, Karen McNally, Dave Melhado, Rich Penney, Steve Reece, Ian Ridley, Simon Smith, Alex Stockbridge, 'Fly' Taylor, Neil Williams; Junior Techs Adrian Adams, Craig Allan, Kurt Barker, Gill Beamish, Darren Burgess, Chris Charlton,

Darren Gillan, Phil Haythornthwaite, Stephen Hill, Dave Lowerson, Scott Mackie, Mick Noy, Stuart O'Donnell, Jethro Pearce, 'Ginge' Robb, Andrew Roberts, Lee Robinson, Jim Slater, Andy Wilkie; SACs Tim Aston, Paul Bacon, Kevin Bealing, Jenny Dempster, David Dyche, Bob Earls, Mike Evans, Justine Helps, Paul Hope, James Landells, Ben Lewis, Nick Lyon, Anthony McCormick, Phil Matthews, Allan Milligan, Andy Murray, Mike Owens, Ken Simpson, Paul Sparrow and Adam Thomas.

A big thanks also to Spike Robertson, Dave Wright, Pete Stern and John Devlin for the many, many helmet and flight-kit fittings and for their patience. And thanks again to Wg Cdr Simon Meade and Sqn Ldr Mike Williams, who were instrumental in getting me my initial access to the team.